THIRD EDITION

ESSENTIAL LIFE SKILLS SERIES

WHAT YOU NEED TO KNOW ABOUT

READING ADS, REFERENCE MATERIALS & LEGAL DOCUMENTS

Carolyn Morton Starkey

Norgina Wright Penn

National Textbook Company
a division of NTC/Contemporary Publishing Company
Lincolnwood, Illinois USA

ACKNOWLEDGMENTS

Alberto-Culver Co., Bold Hold coupon.

Bantam Books, SWEET DREAMS ad. SWEET DREAMS and its associated logo are trademarks of Bantam Books, Inc.

Book-of-the-Month Club, Inc., special offer.

Buick Motor Division, General Motors, owner's manual.

Columbia House Company, Columbia House CD club membership ad.

CONSUMER REPORTS, "Table of Contents," copyright © 1992 by Consumers Union of U.S., Inc., Yonkers, NY 10703–1957. Reprinted by permission from CONSUMER REPORTS, July 1992.

Peter Fitzgerald, drawings on pages 3, 7, and 9.

General Mills, Inc., Cheerios coupon. Used with permission of General Mills, Inc.

Globe Book Company, table of contents. From Henry I. Christ, *Modern Short Biographies,* copyright © 1970, Globe Book Co.

Johnson Publishing Co., *Jet* subscription form.

Keys Group Burger King, coupon.

Lustrasilk Corp., Lustrasilk ad.

McDonald's Corp., job application form.

Michigan Bell Telephone, excerpts from yellow pages.

Newberry Library, Chicago, Illinois, call slip.

J.C. Penney Co., Inc., credit application form.

Scott, Foresman & Co. Excerpts from *Thorndike-Barnhart Advanced Dictionary,* copyright © 1974 by Scott Foresman & Co. Reprinted by permission.

Sharp Electronics Corp., Sharp CB Warranty.

3M Company, Buf-Oxal ad.

The H.W. Wilson Co. *Readers' Guide to Periodical Literature* entries, copyright © 1980, 1981 by the H.W. Wilson Co.

Preface This third edition from the Essential Life Skills Series tells you what you need to know about reading ads, legal documents, and reference materials. Mastering these reading skills and strategies will make you more assertive and self-confident. You will learn to cope better with everyday situations.

This book covers some familiar yet very important materials. You will learn to read, write, and understand:

ads	library reference materials
special offers	dictionaries
credit agreements	tables of contents
warranties	indexes

Throughout the book you will find examples of real ads, credit agreements, warranties, and reference materials, like the ones you see and use everyday.

Each section in this book includes definitions of words that may be new or difficult. Checkup sections help you review what you have learned. There are many opportunities to practice your skills. "Show What You Know" activities offer you the opportunity to apply your new skills.

Because of its flexible format, this book can be used either for self-study or in a group setting with an instructor. The answer key is on perforated pages so that it is easy to remove.

When you have mastered the skills in this book, you will want to develop other skills to become more successful in our modern world. The other books in the Essential Life Skills Series will show you how.

Essential Life Skills Series

What You Need to Know about Reading Labels, Directions & Newspapers
0-8442-5169-0

What You Need to Know about Reading Ads, Reference Materials & Legal Documents 0-8442-5170-4

What You Need to Know about Getting a Job and Filling Out Forms
0-8442-5171-2

What You Need to Know about Reading Signs, Directories, Schedules, Maps, Charts & Graphs 0-8442-5172-0

What You Need to Know about Basic Writing Skills, Letters & Consumer Complaints 0-8442-5173-9

Contents

Reading Critically

Understanding Agreements and Warranties

Reference Strategies

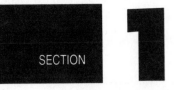

Reading critically

As a buyer, you see or hear many advertising messages each day. These messages often urge you to buy an item because it is marked down. Sometimes a special offer sounds too good to be true. To spend your money wisely, you must be able to read these ads critically. You must also be able to evaluate special offers.

Advertisements

WORDS TO KNOW

bandwagon appeal   the suggestion that you should not miss out on something that lots of other people are doing or buying

consumer   any person who buys and uses up, or consumes, a product

endorse   to give approval, such as the famous football player advertising a well-known soft drink

imply   to suggest something that is not said; for example, implying that a beautiful appearance will lead to fame and fortune

glowing generality   a statement that says something is wonderful or great without giving proof; no specific information

guarantee   a promise of quality or length of use. Often the seller promises to fix or replace a product for a certain length of time.

option   an extra feature, usually for an additional price

symbol   an object that stands for something else, such as beautiful hair for happiness or a car for success

technique   a method or way of doing something

vanity   inflated pride in yourself or your appearance

Do you read the ads in newspapers and magazines? Have you ever bought something simply because it was on sale? Have you ever bought a product because it was endorsed by a superstar? Advertisements are aimed at consumers. They try to make you spend your money. People do buy products because of ads they have seen.

There are many ways you can learn about a product. A friend could recommend a product to you. You could hear about a product at school or work. Sometimes you see something new and decide to buy it. However, most buyers learn about products through ads.

Makers of products spend millions of dollars a year in advertising. They want you to know what they have for sale. They reach you through television and radio commercials. They advertise in newspapers. They advertise in magazines and on billboards.

As a consumer, there are lots of things you need to know about the products you buy. This makes advertising important. Here are some of the things you can learn from ads:

- What an item costs
- What it looks like
- What features it has
- Where you can get it
- How long it can be gotten
- Who makes it
- How it compares to other brands
- Whether it's guaranteed

This type of information is important to you. Sometimes advertisers forget this. They may be advertising a good product, but they don't tell you much about it. Instead, they try to get your attention in other ways. Some advertisers need to use these techniques to sell their product. They know their product does not have a famous brand name. They know the product may lack quality. And they know it may not have sales appeal.

Many sellers of products hire trained people to write their ads. Ad firms use talented people—artists, photographers, writers—to think up ads that will appeal to you. They create ads that they hope will make you want to buy a product. You may see a movie star holding up a jar of Crunchy Nut Peanut Butter. You may buy this peanut butter just because of the famous person. Children are also targets for ads, especially television ads. TV commercials coax children to ask their parents for Fruity-Froot cereal. They want Fruity-Froot because (1) it comes with a toy whistle, (2) it's chocolate coated, and (3) it's the brand "Super Hero" eats. The point is this: All ads try to make you buy a product. Many of these things you may want, need, and can afford. But there are other products that ads *make* you want. You may not need these things.

As a buyer, you must learn to judge ads. You must watch out for advertising techniques. You must learn to look for the facts about what you are buying.

Here are some things you should know about ads:

1. *Some ads are not truthful.* The seller or maker of a product simply does not tell the truth about the product.
2. *Some ads tell half the truth.* This type of advertising misleads the buyer. The ad will *suggest* that something is true. An ad may say just enough to make you say the rest. Sometimes the ad may tell you only half of what you need to know.
3. *Some ads will appeal to your emotions:*
   - your desire to look and feel younger (or older), sexy, handsome
   - your identification with family, friends, country, a TV star
   - memories of "down home" and "the good ol' days"
   - your need to be part of the crowd
4. *Some ads are filled with glowing generalities.* These ads tell you that a product is WONDERFUL, GREAT, FANTASTIC, SUPER, BETTER THAN EVER!
5. *Some ads appeal to your senses,* especially touch and taste. Cotton Cloud Detergent makes your towels feel soft and fluffy. Lemon-Lime Lemonade tastes lemony, limey, and delicious!

Truth in advertising

It's hard to know if some ads tell the truth. The claims made sound good. The ads are *believable*. This is why many consumer groups go after advertisers who print misleading ads. There are now laws that make advertisers tell you more about products. It is too bad that most people learn that an ad has misled them only after they have bought and used a product. Jan used Dawn's Magic Beauty Cream for three weeks. But she could not get rid of her freckles. Tommy Madison threw out his Body Tone FLEX-erciser. After two weeks he hadn't lost the eight inches of fat the ad said he'd lose. And Sarah Hart put her trust in M–24 Special Formula Mouth Wash. She may never know it doesn't help fight colds.

It's even harder to point out the half-truths. A mail-order school might say that it helps its graduates find jobs. It doesn't say that it directs graduates to the local newspaper. A record club may promise you FOUR HIT RECORDS FREE. If you read the ad closely, you learn that you have to *buy* four albums to keep the four *free* ones.

ACTIVITY 1
Reading ads carefully

Answer the questions about the following ads.

LOSE FAT FOREVER

BEFORE

AFTER

You Can Look Like This!

BUY **Fat Off**

No pills, no exercise, no diet.

Fat Off approved by doctors and health clinics.

1. List all the information in this ad that you feel may not be true or may be half true.

_____

_____

2. List all the information in this ad that you feel is definitely true (fact).

_____

_____

1. Does this ad give you the name of the school? _____

2. Does this ad give you a street address (and a building) or just a box number? _____

3. List the home study courses being offered.

_____

_____

_____

4. Which of these courses would probably be best taught in a school with an instructor? Explain.

_____

_____

_____

_____

5. Which of these people would probably answer this ad? More than one answer is possible.

_____ a retired person

_____ a college graduate

_____ a high school dropout

_____ a high school graduate with no vocational skills

_____ an adult who never attended high school

6. Which of these things does the ad _imply_ (make you think something is true without actually saying it)? More than one answer is possible.

_____ When you finish the course, your "Career Certificate" will help you get a job.

_____ Many people who take a career course earn $50,000 a year.

_____ If you are not happy with the course, you will get your money back.

_____ Your $10 will be refunded if you change your mind in the two weeks before the course begins.

_____ Typing is a better career choice than catering.

_____ You don't have to worry about money now. The important thing is to enroll for the current semester. You can always pay later.

_____ The training is like college. (There are semesters, registration, tuition fees.)

Emotional appeals Many ads appeal to your emotions. Some ads may appeal to your vanity. They tell you that you'll look beautiful . . . young . . . sexy . . . handsome. Some ads will touch things dear to you: "Have you talked to your family lately? Call them long distance. It only costs a few pennies." Or "Every American should take stock in America. Buy bonds." Family, friends, country, the flag—all are things that bring out emotions in people. And of course there are strong feelings about things past: homemade goodness, down-home flavor, memories of childhood.

ACTIVITY 2
Reading ads with emotional appeal

Each of the ads below appeals to your emotions. Is it your vanity? Your intelligence? Your good looks? Answer the questions about each ad.

INTELLIGENT
        SHOPPERS...

BUY

SUPER SHINE

FURNITURE POLISH

They've compared brands-
They know **SUPER SHINE**
outshines them all!

What does this ad appeal to?

————

(a) Your need to feel your house is clean?
(b) Your need to feel smart?
(c) Your vanity?

Feel beautiful. . .
    Look beautiful. . .
        Be beautiful. . .

USE

*Hair
Color
Magic*

The shampoo and hair color
for the beautiful you. . .

What does this ad appeal to?

————

(a) Your need to belong
(b) Your intelligence
(c) Your vanity

ACTIVITY 3
Reading ads with emotional appeal—"the famous person"

An ad that has a lot of emotional appeal is the famous person ad. Sometimes your favorite television star will endorse a product. You like this person. You are a loyal fan. You transfer your emotions for the person to the product. If "Michael Borden" eats it, wears it, or drinks it, you will too. Maybe if you use Bright White toothpaste, you'll have white, attractive teeth like "Christine Fargate." The next ad is a famous person ad. Answer the questions about this ad.

1. Why do you think this famous person was asked to do this ad? _____

2. This ad is filled with OPINIONS—what a person *thinks* about the product. List all the opinions you

   find in this ad. _____

3. Which of the following statements best summarizes this ad? _____

   (a) Lyle Fetty uses PST in his car, and you should use it in yours.

   (b) Whatever is good for Lyle Fetty's car is good for everybody's car because he's a famous race driver.

   (c) PST will make your car run well enough for the Indiana 600.

ACTIVITY 4
Reading ads with emotional appeal—"get on the bandwagon"

Some ads appeal to your need to follow the crowd. Many people call this the bandwagon ad. The ad makes you feel left out—not in with what everyone else is doing. Read the following ad carefully. Then answer the questions about it.

1. List all the words and phrases that appeal to a person's desire to join the crowd. _____

2. How does this ad use *art* to help convince you that you should "get on the bandwagon"? —————

3. Do you think that buying something because everyone else seems to be is a good reason? Explain why you feel the way you do. ————————————————————

Glowing generalities

When you read an ad, you should expect to find out more about a product. Has the brand been tested? If so, by whom? What is being said? Are there facts that can be checked out? How does the product compare to other brands? What does it cost? How long does it last? Sometimes, instead of facts, ads contain a lot of general statements. If all the generalities were taken out of the ad, you would find that the ad told you very little, if anything, about the product.

ACTIVITY 5
Reading ads— specific information or glowing generality

Read the following ad and the statements from this ad. Do the statements contain specific information or glowing generalities?

**THE NEW FLEETLINE
THE CAR OF THE FUTURE**

▶ Improved steering
▶ More space than ever
▶ V-8 engine
▶ Vinyl roof
▶ Air conditioning
▶ Tremendous mileage

Now is the time for spectacular savings on this year's spectacular car. You have a variety of options and colors to choose from. You have a chance to ride the most sensational automobile on the road, the Fleetline—Tomorrow's car—today.

	Specific information	Glowing generality
1. The Fleetline has a V-8 engine.	—————	—————
2. The Fleetline gives you tremendous mileage.	—————	—————
3. This car has "more space than ever."	—————	—————
4. The Fleetline comes with a vinyl roof.	—————	—————
5. The Fleetline comes in a variety of colors.	—————	—————
6. The Fleetline is this year's spectacular car.	—————	—————

ACTIVITY 6
Evaluating popular advertisements: Finding out what types of ads appeal to you

In this activity you will look at several ads. These ads are for famous products. Many of the ads you may have read before. You will be asked questions about each of these ads. These questions will help you find out (1) if you are able to identify advertising techniques, (2) if you can separate facts from opinions, and (3) what type(s) of ads appeal to you. Be prepared to discuss your answers in class.

Read this ad for Sweet Dreams books. Answer the questions about it.

1. What type of person do you think this ad appeals to? _____

2. Does it appeal to you? Explain why or why not.

_____

3. Give examples of words or phrases in the ad that show these types of emotional appeal.

   (a) a person's need to be popular _____

   (b) a person's desire to be beautiful _____

   (c) a person's identification with dreams and fantasies instead of reality _____

Doin' the "Curl" with Lustra-Curl®

Don't waste another minute! Get up and start doin' it up! Get a *Lustra-Curl* cause it's the *"real curl."* *Lustra-Curl* gives you versatility for lots of styles. Curls to suit your fancy. Big Ones. Long Ones. Fancy Ones. Perfect curls that feel as good as they look. Ask your stylist about *Lustra-Curl* and the finest in after-care products. You'll have all the fun . . .

Lustrasilk

LUSTRASILK 1982
P.O. BOX 334, MPLS MN 55440

Look at the ad for a hair care product on page 11. Read it carefully. This ad uses pictures of people for much of its appeal. Answer the questions about the ad.

1. What emotion does this ad appeal to? ——————————————
   _____

2. Make a list of the glowing generalities in this ad.
   _____
   _____
   _____
   _____
   _____
   _____

3. Does this ad contain any facts about the product? If so, what are they?
   _____
   _____
   _____
   _____

4. What reasons does the ad give for you to buy this product?
   _____
   _____
   _____
   _____

Read this ad. Separate the facts in it from the opinions.

- "Zits are the Pits."

- Buf-Oxal is a benzoyl peroxide gel.

- Buf-Oxal is gentle.

- You will be surprised at how quickly Buf-Oxal will clean up your pimples, blackheads, and blemishes.

- Buf-Oxal is available in 5% and 10% strengths.

- Buf-Oxal is water-based.

Facts

_____

_____

_____

_____

_____

Opinions

_____

_____

_____

_____

CHECK YOUR UNDERSTANDING OF ADVERTISEMENTS

Here are some words you should know when you are reading ads critically. Find the correct word for each of the statements below.

guarantee   endorse   vanity

bandwagon appeal   optional   glowing generality

1. My new watch came with a _____ against defects for six months.

2. The ad for skin cream says that your skin will feel great after using the cream. This statement is a

_____ .

3. Ads for certain kinds of sweaters or jackets appeal to a person's _____ .

4. Ads for certain products say that since so many other people are buying the product, you should

too. This is called a _____ .

5. Certain features, like air conditioning, are _____ on a new car.

6. During baseball season, famous players often _____ certain products.

List the advertising techniques used in each of the following quotations from ads. Refer to p.   2 for a list of the advertising techniques you have been studying.

7. "Driving is a new sensation . . . America's most popular sports car. Hot stuff." _____

8. "Don't miss this wonderful product." _____

9. "Lose 10 pounds in one week without dieting!" _____

10. "Sheets that are soft, smooth, fragrant." _____

14

SHOW WHAT YOU KNOW . . .

About Advertisements

Find at least two (2) examples of each type of ad listed below. Number them 1–8, but do not label them. On a separate sheet of paper, write the numbers 1–8 and identify each ad. This is your answer key.

1. Lies and half-truths

2. Bandwagon appeal

3. Emotional appeal

4. Glowing generalities

During class, exchange ads with a partner. Attempt to identify the ads on a separate sheet of paper. After you are finished, exchange answer keys. Correct your answers.

Special offers

The consumer's world is filled with sales offers. Many offers are found in newspapers and magazines. Others come to you in the mail. These special offers can mean savings to you. However, you must read these offers very carefully. How much of a savings will you get? What will your responsibilities be?

Reading magazine subscription offers

With a subscription you can get magazines through the mail at discount prices. Magazine subscriptions are often for one or two years. Sometimes magazines have special offers for short periods. These offers give very low prices. They are for *new* subscribers. A subscriber's rate will be below the newsstand price.

When you read subscription offers, there are three things you want to know: (1) how long your subscription will last (or how many issues you will get), (2) what the subscription will cost, and (3) how much of a savings you will get.

ACTIVITY 7

Interpreting magazine subscription offers

Read the following magazine subscription offer. Decide whether the statements about the offer are TRUE (T) or FALSE (F).

FOR THE 52 WEEKS OF CHRISTMAS

The one Christmas gift that's
always the right size,
shape, color and price.

JET

An Attractive Card Announces Your Gift

First one-year subscription $24.00
Each additional subscription $20.00.
Offer Good in United States Only

Your Name_____
Please Print

Address_____ Apt. #_____

City_____

State_____ Zip_____

_____My own order   _____Renewal with Gifts

Payment Enclosed $_____   Bill me_____

Mail To: JET Gift Subscriptions, 820 South Michigan Ave., Chicago, Illinois 60605

Name_____
Please Print

Address_____ Apt. #_____

City_____

State_____ Zip_____

Gift Card From_____

Name_____
Please Print

Address_____ Apt. #_____

City_____

State_____ Zip_____

Gift Card From_____

Name_____
Please Print

Address_____ Apt. #_____

City_____

State_____ Zip_____

Gift Card From_____

_____ **1.** This is a weekly magazine.

_____ **2.** You may have a gift card sent with gift subscriptions.

_____ **3.** Your first subscription will cost $24.00.

_____ **4.** Each additional subscription will cost $20.00.

_____ **5.** Canadians can take advantage of this offer for a slightly higher cost.

Reading music club offers

Music club memberships appeal to both teenagers and adults. These offers require specific reading skills. You may be able to save money on recordings. To get the special prices, however, you usually must agree to make more purchases.

When you read these offers, read for specific details. Know how many more purchases you have to make. Read to understand what kind of discount, if any, you will get as a member. Know what kind of musical choices you will have. Will you be able to select classical music? country? dance pop? R & B? hard rock? rap? Read to find out what you must do if you ever want to cancel your membership. All this information should be somewhere in the club membership offer.

ACTIVITY 8
Reading a CD offer for details

Read the CD (compact disc) offer on the next page. Then answer the questions below.

1. How much must you send to join the Columbia House CD Club? _____

2. How often will you receive offers of main selections? _____ of special selections? _____

3. If you want the main selection, what do you do? _____

4. If you want an alternate CD, what do you do? _____

5. How many days do you have to make your choice? _____

6. If you receive a CD before this time, can it be returned? _____

7. Will you get full credit? _____

8. Who pays shipping charges? _____

9. What is the regular club price for CDs? _____ the extra bonus offer price? _____

10. When can you cancel your membership? _____

Reading book club offers

Book club membership offers are a lot like record and tape club offers. Best sellers, like hit records, are offered to new members at special low prices. Once you accept a membership offer, you must purchase a certain number of books within a certain amount of time. You may have six months to make these purchases. Sometimes you may have as long as a year. You must read carefully for the specific details of the offer. Know what you're agreeing to do.

ACTIVITY 9
Reading a book club offer for details

Read this book club offer. Answer the questions about this offer.

Choose any 4 for $2.

You simply agree to buy 4 books within the next two years.

Book-of-the-Month Club, Inc., Camp Hill, Pennsylvania 17012   A304-10-1

Please enroll me as a member of Book-of-the-Month Club and send me the 4 books I've listed below, billing me $2, plus shipping and handling charges. I agree to buy 4 more books during the next two years. A shipping and handling charge is added to each shipment.

Indicate by number the four books you want

Mr.
Mrs. _____ 2-04
Miss   (Please print plainly)

Address_____ Apt _____

City_____

State_____ Zip_____

Prices generally higher in Canada

BOOK-OF-THE-MONTH CLUB
America's Bookstore® since 1926.

Benefits of Membership. Membership in the Book-of-the-Month Club begins with your choice of 4 of today's best books for $2. Because our prices are generally lower than the publishers' prices, you will save throughout your membership on the finest new titles. In fact, the longer you remain a member, the greater your savings can be. Our Book-Dividend® plan, for which you become eligible after a brief trial enrollment, offers savings from 50% to 75% off the publishers' prices on art books, reference works, classics, books on cooking and crafts, literary sets and other contemporary works of enduring value. Nevertheless, all Book-of-the-Month Club books are equal in quality to the publishers' originals; they are not condensed versions or cheaply made reprints.

As a member you will receive the Book-of-the-Month Club News® 15 times a year (about every 3½ weeks). Every issue reviews a Selection and 150 other books that we call Alternates, which are carefully chosen by our editors. If you want the Selection, do nothing. It will be shipped to you automatically. If you want one or more Alternates—or no book at all—indicate your decision on the Reply Form and return it by the specified date. *Return Privilege:* If the *News* is delayed and you receive the Selection without having had 10 days to notify us, you may return it for credit at our expense. *Cancellations:* Membership may be discontinued, either by you or by the Club, at any time after you have bought 4 additional books. Join today. With savings and choices like these, no wonder Book-of-the-Month Club is America's Bookstore.

1. If Book-of-the-Month Club accepts your application, how many books will you receive? _____

2. What will these books cost?_____

3. How many days do you have to decide if you want to keep the main selection? _____

4. If you accept the books, are there any other charges? _____

5. How often will you receive the Book-of-the-Month Club news? _____

6. By accepting this offer, how many books are you agreeing to buy during the next two years? _____

7. If you do not want the Selection of the Month, what do you do? _____

Coupon savings

Many ads have savings coupons. You can use these discount coupons for savings on a lot of products. First, you clip the coupon. You then redeem it at the time of your purchase. Some coupons will be for refunds. To get a refund you may have to show proof-of-purchase. Proof-of-purchase can be a label, a price code, or a cash register receipt. Shopping with coupons can result in savings. Sometimes there's something free with your purchase. However, coupons are still a form of advertising. Read all coupons carefully. Sometimes a savings may not be on a product you need. Coupons have expiration dates, too. You must use a coupon before it expires.

ACTIVITY 10
Reading coupon offers

Answer the questions about the following coupon offers.

1. What two products can you buy with these coupons? _____

_____

2. Do you have to buy a certain size? _____

3. Can you redeem these coupons for cash without making a purchase? _____

4. Do these coupons have expiration dates? _____

ACTIVITY 11

Reading refund and free coupon offers

Answer the questions about each of the following offers.

1. How much is this coupon worth? _____

2. Do you have to purchase certain items in order to use this coupon? _____

3. If your purchase comes to 80¢, will you receive change from this coupon? _____

4. How many Key Group Burger Kings are there? _____

GET A $2.00 CASH REFUND

BUY: Any 3 **different** of these brands:
Betty Crocker® SuperMoist® cake mix, Creamy Deluxe® or MiniMorsels Frosting, Gold Medal® or Red Band® Flour (5 lbs or larger), Betty Crocker® Brownie Mix (Frosted, Chocolate Chip, Walnut, Supreme, or German Chocolate), Betty Crocker® Muffin Mix.

SEND: 1) The UPC symbols (see sample) from your three purchases
2) This mail-in certificate.

MAIL TO: General Mills, Inc.
Box 5237
Minneapolis, MN 55460

RECEIVE: Cash Refund of $2.00 by mail.

MAIL-IN CASH REFUND CERTIFICATE

Name _____

Address _____

City _____

State _____ Zip _____

OFFER EXPIRES MAY 31, 1988

Mechanical reproduction, facsimile, purchase or sale or other dissemination of this offer without the written consent of General Mills, Inc. are prohibited. This certificate must accompany your request. Void where taxed, regulated or prohibited. Offer limited to one refund per group, organization or address. Please allow up to 6 weeks per shipment. Qualifiers will not be returned for duplicate requests or requests from outside stated area. Offer good only in VA, WVA, NC, SC, GA, FL, TN.

1. What do you get when you mail in this coupon? _____

2. Do you have to send in proof-of-purchase? If so, what do you send? _____

3. What is the value of this offer? _____

4. Where do you mail this coupon? _____

5. How long do you have to wait for your cash? _____

6. What is the expiration date on this offer? _____

CHECK YOUR UNDERSTANDING OF SPECIAL OFFERS

Here are some words to know when you are reading a special offer. Find the correct word or phrase for each of the sentences below.

redeem   coupon   expiration date
discount   refund   obligation

1. A _____ for 10¢ off on the price of crackers was in the daily newspaper.

2. The _____ of the coupon was March 31, 1993.

3. When I joined a book club, I had a(n) _____ to purchase 4 additional books.

4. The electronic toy I purchased included a coupon for a $5 _____ .

5. I like to buy things at _____ stores because they offer products at lower prices.

6. I decided to buy a certain brand of crackers because I had a coupon to _____ .

Decide whether the following statements are TRUE (T) or FALSE (F).

_____ 7. When a book club offers a number of books for an introductory low price, you can get these books without buying anything else from the club at that time.

_____ 8. Record and tape and book clubs usually automatically send you the selection of the month.

_____ 9. Magazine and newspaper subscriptions cost less than the newsstand price.

_____ 10. Coupons for food products never have expiration dates.

SHOW WHAT YOU KNOW . . .

About Special Offers

Design a coupon for a product that you create.
Include all of the important information that a coupon should have.

Under- standing agreements and warranties

Have you ever returned an item for a refund, leased a piece of equipment, or made a credit card purchase? Chapter 5 explores consumer agreements and contracts and the warranties that come with certain purchases. You will study sales and service agreements. You will also study credit agreements. You will interpret the terms used in these agreements. This chapter presents a number of warranties for your review. It includes a cassette player warranty and a new car warranty.

Agreements and contracts

WORDS TO KNOW

annual   each year

balance   the amount you owe after payment; amount left

collateral   property promised to a creditor, such as a car or furniture, if a debt is not paid

co-maker   second person agreeing to credit terms; also known as co-applicant, co-signer, or co-borrower

conditions   terms; special circumstances

consent   agree to; give permission

consumer   buyer or borrower

contract   legal agreement

credit   ability to buy or borrow and pay at a later date

credit terms   how you are to pay for a credit purchase or repay a loan

creditor   person or business giving you credit; lender; seller

debts   bills you owe; obligations

default   nonpayment; failure to pay as agreed

delinquent   late

disclosure   to make known; to state in writing; a written statement of the terms of a loan or credit agreement

down payment   money paid in advance on credit purchase

entitle   give the right to; permit; allow

finance charge   cost of having credit; monthly charge on credit agreement, usually used on charge card agreements

installment   monthly payment

(continued)

interest   cost of credit, usually used in loan agreements

landlord   person who owns and rents out a house, apartment, or building

lease   a rent agreement

liability   legal responsibility

lien   a legal claim on your property for nonpayment of a debt

option   choice

percentage rate   interest or finance charges stated as a percentage of what you owe

retailer   seller or merchant; person or business giving credit

sue   take to court; take legal action against

tenant   person renting an apartment, a house, or a building

title   legal document proving ownership

violate   fail to keep an agreement

The special words used for contracts and agreements are very technical. You will see these words in credit agreements. You will see them in rent agreements. You will see them in employment agency contracts, too. You will also see these words in sales and service agreements. For example, retail stores often post rules about returns and refunds. There may be terms on the receipt of your car repair bill. There may be terms on the back of your dry-cleaning ticket. (Dry cleaners take very little responsibility for damaged clothes.) Some of these agreements do not require your signature. But they are still agreements. When you buy goods or pay for services, you are accepting the terms of the seller. Study the *Words to Know* carefully. They are the words you will see and use. Your understanding of them can help you protect your rights.

ACTIVITY 1
Using credit terms

The words below are often found in credit agreements. Use these words to complete the statements below.

disclosure   percentage rate   debts
co-maker   delinquent   default
creditor   interest   installment
down payment

1. Ira Atkins just got a(n) _____ loan for a new car.

2. Of course, Ira will have to pay _____ on this loan.

3. The annual _____ is stated in the credit agreement.

4. Ira had to read a _____ statement before signing the credit agreement.

5. The _____ must always let you know the terms of credit.

6. There was a _____ required.

7. Ira's wife, Ellen, was _____ of the loan.

8. Ellen will have to repay the loan should Ira _____ .

9. The _____ charges are $5 per month for each late payment.

10. When Ira and Ellen applied for the loan, they had to list all their _____ .

ACTIVITY 2
Reading credit agreements

Each of the statements below was taken from a credit agreement. The language is very technical. Which of the statements listed below means the same as the statement from the agreement?

1.
> If an installment is not paid within 10 days after it is due, a delinquent charge of $5 will be paid by the buyer . . .

_____ a. If you are late with your monthly payment, you must pay $5.
_____ b. If you are more than 10 days late with a payment, you must pay a "late charge."
_____ c. If you are more than 10 days late with your monthly payment, you must pay $5 in late charges.

2.

> For the purpose of securing payment of the obligation, creditor holds title to 1993 Buick as collateral and shall have a security interest in said property until said obligation is fully paid . . .

_____ **a.** Your title will be held until you pay your debt.

_____ **b.** You can hold the title to your property, but if you fail to pay this bill, the lender will demand the title to your car.

_____ **c.** To be sure you pay this bill, the lender will hold the registration papers to your car until the bill is paid in full.

3.

> Debtor will not sell or offer to sell or otherwise transfer ownership of the collateral without written consent of creditor . . .

_____ **a.** You can sell the collateral, for example, a car.

_____ **b.** The lender can sell or transfer the collateral (car) if he or she lets you know in writing.

_____ **c.** As the borrower, you can't sell the collateral (car) unless the person holding the collateral or title to the collateral gives you written permission.

4.

> As co-signer of this agreement, I am aware of my liability and I hereby authorize you to obtain credit information relative to me.

_____ **a.** As co-maker of a loan, you are responsible for the loan if it is not paid.

_____ **b.** You have agreed to share the responsibility for a debt.

_____ **c.** You have signed to have your credit checked and to share the responsibility for a debt.

ACTIVITY 3

Using agreements and contract words

Match the words on the left with their meanings on the right.

_____ **A.** lease

_____ **B.** balance

_____ **C.** consumer

_____ **D.** entitle

_____ **E.** landlord

_____ **F.** default

_____ **G.** obligation

_____ **H.** annual

_____ **I.** credit

_____ **J.** conditions

1. failure to pay as agreed

2. amount you owe

3. rent agreement

4. terms

5. buy-now and pay-later plan

6. each year

7. buyer

8. allow

9. apartment owner

10. responsibility

ACTIVITY 4

Reading terms on charge accounts

Many people make purchases by using credit cards or opening charge accounts. The law requires that *all* creditors provide buyers with disclosure information. This means companies offering charge accounts must give you the terms of your agreement in writing. This information will come with your application for credit. Sometimes it is separate from the application. When you put your signature on a credit agreement, you are accepting all of the terms in the agreement. The J. C. Penney revolving credit agreement on the next two pages appears on the *back* of a Penney's Credit Application.

Answer TRUE (T) or FALSE (F) to the following statements about the credit terms.

_____ 1. You will not have to pay finance charges if you make regular monthly installment payments.

_____ 2. Payments must be made within 30 days of the billing date.

_____ 3. If your average daily balance is $28.50, the finance charge is 50¢.

_____ 4. If you make a $10 charge purchase on March 2 and a $150 charge on March 28, your finance charge for the month of March will be based on an average daily balance that does include the $150.

_____ 5. When you pay 1.75% in finance charges each month, you are paying 21% in finance charges each year.

_____ 6. You must pay the minimum payment each month.

_____ 7. You may pay more than the minimum monthly payment, but not less.

_____ 8. If you owe $210, your monthly payment will be $13.

_____ 9. Your signature gives J. C. Penney permission to investigate your credit record.

_____ 10. Unpaid finance or insurance charges are included when an average daily balance is figured.

YOUR JCPenney RETAIL INSTALLMENT CREDIT AGREEMENT
(Revolving Credit Agreement)

JCP-9501 (Rev. 1/91)

In this agreement, *you* and *your* mean anyone who has applied for and been accepted for a JCPenney Credit Account. *We, us,* and *our* mean the J.C. Penney Company, Inc., 14841 North Dallas Parkway, Dallas, TX 75240-6760.

Credit Bureau Reports — To check the information on your application, we may get a report about you from a credit bureau. When you have an account, we may get a credit report to update our records or to decide whether to give you additional credit. Ask us and we will tell you if we requested a credit report and give you the name and address of the credit bureau.

Types of Charges — The purchase of any merchandise or service may be added to your account as a Regular Charge. Certain merchandise (identified in our stores and catalogs) may be added to your account as a Major Purchase Charge.

Promise to Pay — You agree to pay for all authorized charges to your account as well as any charges from which you receive a benefit.

Payment Requirements — When you have a balance, you agree to pay at least the minimum payment amount due each month. **You can pay your entire balance at any time.** Your required payment may include any past due amounts, late charges, and returned check fees. Your required payment may also include any insurance premiums if your policy is billed with your account.

Failure to Pay — If you do not pay on time, we can require that you make immediate payment of your entire balance unless you have rights by state law to correct your non-payment.

We may use an outside attorney to collect your account. If there is a lawsuit and you lose, you agree to pay reasonable attorney's fees, plus court costs, as permitted by the law in your state.

Annual Fee — There is no annual fee on your JCPenney Credit Account.

Grace Period — You do not pay any finance charge if there is no previous balance or if credits and payments made within 25 days of the current billing date equal the balance at the beginning of the period.

Finance Charge — Finance charge not in excess of that permitted by law will be assessed on the outstanding balance(s) from month to month. We figure the finance charge by applying the periodic rate(s) to the Average Daily Balance(s) of your account.

Balance Calculation Method — Average Daily Balance: Current purchases are included in the calculation except in the states of ME, MA, MN, MT, NE, and NM.

- To get the Average Daily Balance, we take the beginning balance each day, add new purchases, and subtract payments and credits. In ME, MA, MN, MT, NE, and NM, current purchases are not included during the billing period in which they were made. In AR, CA, HI, LA, MS, ND, and PA, unpaid finance charges from a previous billing period are not included.

- We add all the daily balances for the billing period and divide the total by the number of days in that period. This gives us the Average Daily Balance.

- We figure the Average Daily Balance separately for a Regular Charge balance and a Major Purchase balance. We add these Average Daily Balances to get the account's total Average Daily Balance.

Excluded from finance charge calculation are insurance premiums, returned check fees, and late payment charges.

Regular Charges — If you have a Regular Charge balance, you agree to make at least a minimum payment each month as listed below:

IF YOUR REGULAR CHARGE BALANCE IS:	YOUR MONTHLY PAYMENT IS:
$ 20.00 or less	Balance
20.01 — 100	$ 20
100.01 — 200	30
200.01 — 250	35
250.01 — 300	40
300.01 — 350	45
350.01 — 400	50
400.01 — 450	55
450.01 — 550	60
550.01 — 600	65
Over $600	11% of the balance rounded down to the whole dollar.

Major Purchase Charges — If you have a Major Purchase balance, you agree to pay at least a fixed amount each month. This amount is based on your highest Major Purchase balance. Even if you reduce your balance, your monthly payment will remain the same until that balance is paid.

IF YOUR HIGHEST MAJOR PURCHASE BALANCE IS:	YOUR MONTHLY PAYMENT IS:
$200.00 — 240	$ 15
240.01 — 270	16

For balances between $270.01 and $1,000, the monthly payment of $16 is $1 more for each additional $30 or less.

For balances over $1,000, the monthly payment is 4% of the balance rounded down to the whole dollar.

Our Rights — Warning: We can change our credit terms at any time. We will notify you in advance of any such changes as required by law. Our new terms may be applied to the existing balance on your account unless prohibited by law. We can limit or cancel your credit privileges. All JCPenney credit cards belong to us, and you must return them at our request.

We give up any lien the law gives us automatically for work performed by us or materials installed by us on real property used or expected to be used as your principal residence. If you live in Florida, we will keep a security interest in any items charged to your account, except for those items that are considered real property under state law.

If You Move — You must notify us promptly if you move. If your new residence is in another state, our terms in that state will apply. If you move outside the U.S. (50 states), our standard credit account terms will apply.

Information About You and Your Account, and Telephone Communications
We may share information about you with a member of JCPenney's family of companies or in activities conducted by the JCPenney family of companies. We may give information about your account to credit bureaus and where required or permitted by law. Your telephone conversations with employees or agents of JCPenney's family of companies may be monitored for quality assurance purposes, and your use of your account will signify your consent to such monitoring.

Advertisements and Solicitations — We send advertisements with billing statements, in separate mailings, and by telephone solicitation, which you agree to receive. However, you can tell us at the credit desk in any JCPenney store or by sending a note to the Credit Service Center address shown on your billing statement, that you do not want to receive these advertisements and telephone solicitations.

Finance Charge Rates — The periodic rate for your state is listed below:

Residence	Periodic Rate	ANNUAL PERCENTAGE RATE	Portion of Average Daily Balance to Which Applied	Minimum Monthly FINANCE CHARGE
AL	1.75% 1.5%	21% 18%	$750 or less over $750	50¢
AK	1.5% .79%	18% 9.48%	$1,000 or less over $1,000	50¢
CO, DE, GA, ID, IL, KY, LA, MS, MT, NV, NM, OH, OK, SD, UT, WY	1.75%	21%	Entire	50¢
FL	1.5%	18%	Entire	50¢
NE	1.75% 1.5%	21% 18%	$500 or less over $500	None
ND	1.5%	18%	Entire	None
WV	1.5% 1.0%	18% 12%	$750 or less over $750	50¢
Outside U.S. — 50 States	1.75%	21%	Entire	50¢

There is no minimum monthly finance charge if you have only a Major Purchase balance.

Returned Check Fee — If any check sent to us as payment on your account and/or for insurance premiums is returned unpaid by your bank, we may charge you a reasonable returned check fee.

Late Payment Charge — This applies to you if you live in AL, FL, GA, ID, IL, KY, LA, MS, MT, NV, OH, SD, WV, or outside the U.S. If we do not receive your required payment within two consecutive billing periods, we may assess a late payment charge. This charge is 5% of the late payment (excluding any insurance premiums and returned check fees), but not more than $5.00 ($3.00 in Ohio).

Taxes on Finance Charge — If you live in MS any finance charge assessed on your account is subject to the MS state sales tax. The current rate of that tax is 6%.

Transfer of Your Account — We may transfer your account and our rights under this agreement. The transferee receiving such transfer will be entitled to your account payments and will have all of our rights under this agreement.

NOTICE: See reverse side for important information regarding your rights to dispute billing errors.

To find out if there have been any changes to the credit terms of this agreement, write to the JCPenney Credit Department, P.O. Box 300, Dallas, TX 75221.

NOTICE: ANY HOLDER OF THIS CONSUMER CREDIT CONTRACT IS SUBJECT TO ALL CLAIMS AND DEFENSES WHICH THE DEBTOR COULD ASSERT AGAINST THE SELLER OF GOODS OR SERVICES OBTAINED PURSUANT HERETO OR WITH THE PROCEEDS HEREOF. RECOVERY HEREUNDER BY THE DEBTOR SHALL NOT EXCEED AMOUNTS PAID BY THE DEBTOR HEREUNDER.

ILLINOIS — Residents of Illinois may contact the Illinois Commissioner of Banks and Trust Companies for comparative information on interest rates, charges, fees, and grace periods (State of Illinois — CIP, P.O. Box 10181, Springfield, IL 62791 or telephone 1-800-634-5452).

OHIO — The Ohio laws against discrimination require that all creditors make credit equally available to all creditworthy customers, and that credit reporting agencies maintain separate credit histories on each individual upon request. The Ohio Civil Rights Commission administers compliance with this law.

NOTICE TO THE BUYER: Do not sign this credit agreement before you read it or if it contains any blank spaces. You are entitled to a completely filled in copy of the credit agreement when you sign it. Keep it to protect your legal rights. You have the right to pay in advance the full amount due.

Sign here and keep this Retail Installment Credit Agreement (Revolving Credit Agreement) for your records.
J.C. Penney Company, Inc.

Ted L. Spurlock

Ted L. Spurlock
Senior Vice President
Director of Financial Services

Applicant's Signature _____ Date _____

Co-Applicant's Signature _____ Date _____

Protect Your JCPenney Account With Credit Insurance

DISABILITY AND UNEMPLOYMENT BENEFITS —This insurance protection pays your minimum monthly payment on the covered balance of your JCPenney Credit Account if you the billed accountholder, while insured, become totally disabled or involuntarily unemployed [strike (except Illinois), laid-off, fired] for over 30 days. You're paid benefits from the date your disability or unemployment begins until your covered balance is paid off or you are no longer disabled or involuntarily unemployed. To collect unemployment benefits you must be employed 30 hours per week for four consecutive weeks at the time you become unemployed. "Covered balance" is the outstanding balance on your account, both Regular Charges and Major Purchase Charges, up to $5,000. The covered balance does not include other insurance premiums, nor does it include additional purchases made after the date of loss.

LIFE BENEFITS — If you or your spouse die, it pays the covered balance on your JCPenney Credit Account, up to $5,000. Your spouse is only insured for the life insurance coverage and not for disability and unemployment coverage.

COST — For the months you have an outstanding balance, THE COST IS 65¢ PER $100 (59¢ PER $100 IN ALABAMA, 73¢ PER $100 IN OKLAHOMA) OF THAT COVERED BALANCE. EXAMPLE: If your cost is 65¢ and your covered balance is $200, an insurance charge of $1.30 will appear on your account statement. You're not charged when you owe no balance. No finance charge will be added to your charged premium. Your insurance premium will be paid for you whenever you're receiving benefits.

ELIGIBILITY AND TERMS — The billed accountholder must be under age 66 to enroll (under age 65 for Illinois residents; under age 70 for Oklahoma residents). The insurance effective date is stated on the certificate or policy to be sent to you. Disability and Unemployment coverages stop and the cost of insurance may change at age 66 (all benefits cease at age 66 in DE, FL, NE, NM and WY; life benefits cease at age 70 in Oklahoma). Insurance stops when you're 120 days late paying the minimum payment on your account, the day your account is closed, this group is cancelled or when the accountholder dies. If, after you receive the certificate of insurance, you do not wish to keep the coverage, send the certificate back to us within 30 days from the effective date. We will credit your account for any premium charged for this coverage. ACCEPTING THIS INSURANCE WILL NOT AFFECT WHETHER OR NOT YOU RECEIVE A JCPENNEY CREDIT ACCOUNT. CM200(1/85), CM300(1/85), CI302(8/85) IL, NM. This opportunity is available only to residents of AL, AK, CO, DE, FL, GA, ID, IL, KY, LA, MS, MT, NE, NV, NM, ND, OH, OK, SD, UT, WV, and WY.

Coverage is issued by J.C. Penney Life Insurance Company, and J.C. Penney Casualty Insurance Company, Administrative Offices: 2700 W. Plano Parkway, Plano, TX 75075-8200, each of which is solely responsible for its own financial condition and contractual obligations.

JCP-2201 (Rev. 11/91)

⌐ PLEASE DETACH HERE — FOLD DOWN TO ARROWS BELOW

ACTIVITY 5
Reading agreements

In this activity you will read terms and conditions from various sales and service agreements. They are terms from rental agencies, garages, dry cleaners. Sometimes these terms are posted for customers to read. Sometimes terms or conditions will be on a receipt or sales slip. Your initials or signature may be required. It depends on the type of agreement and the laws in your state. Look at the box below. It contains a list of items that usually come with limits or conditions. Match each of the conditions stated below the box with an item from the box. Use the *letter* that corresponds to the correct item. A letter may be used more than once.

a. Car Rental Agreement	**d.** Rent-a-Tool Agreement
b. Magazine Subscriber's Contract	**e.** Department Store Refund Policy
c. Car Repair Bill	**f.** Dry-Cleaning Ticket

1. "You or your employees may operate this vehicle for purposes of testing, inspection, or delivery at my risk . . ." _____

2. "In laundering we cannot guarantee colors, shrinkage, or synthetic materials . . ." _____

3. "We cannot assume responsibility for buckles, buttons, suedes, leathers . . ." _____

4. "The renter agrees that the motor vehicle leased to him shall not be operated by any person under the influence of narcotics or intoxicants . . ." _____

5. "A mechanic's lien is acknowledged on this vehicle to secure the amount of repairs . . ." _____

6. "Notify lessor immediately if equipment does not function properly or no refund allowance will be made." _____

7. "Merchandise may be returned within 10 days if in salable condition as new." _____

8. "This policy does not apply to 'as is,' 'final sales,' or 'custom-made' merchandise." _____

9. "Please enter my subscription for the following magazines. I understand that it will take 8 to 12 weeks for normal service for these publications to begin." _____

10. "Vehicle shall NOT be used to tow a trailer or any other vehicle . . ." _____

Choose the best answer to complete the following statements.

_____ 1. The phrase "annual finance charge" means
   a. the weekly charge.
   b. the monthly charge.
   c. the yearly charge.

_____ 2. If you pay your whole bill each month for items you have charged,
   a. you will not have to pay a finance charge.
   b. you still have to pay a finance charge.
   c. you still must make installment payments.

_____ 3. Your monthly payments usually depend on
   a. the fixed amount you have agreed to pay.
   b. the interest rate.
   c. the amount of credit you are allowed.

_____ 4. Installment payments are usually made
   a. monthly.
   b. weekly.
   c. yearly.

_____ 5. A liability is a
   a. type of agreement.
   b. legal responsibility.
   c. rent agreement.

_____ 6. "This policy does not apply to sale merchandise" might be part of a statement in a
   a. dry cleaners.
   b. department store.
   c. car rental agency.

_____ 7. A lease is a
   a. credit agreement.
   b. rent agreement.
   c. type of warranty.

_____ 8. When you leave collateral for a debt, you
   a. agree to repay the loan.
   b. leave the property or the title to property with the lender.
   c. get another person to share the debt.

_____ 9. When you are late with an installment payment, you are
   a. delinquent.
   b. co-maker.
   c. in agreement.

_____ 10. Charge applications ask you
   a. your religion.
   b. your race.
   c. your annual salary.

SHOW WHAT YOU KNOW . . .

About Agreements and Contracts

Rewrite the following statements from a credit card agreement in your own words.

1. If I do not make at least the minimum required monthly payment when due, Shears Company may declare my entire balance immediately due and payable.

   _____

   _____

   _____

2. Shears has a security interest under the Uniform Commercial Code in all merchandise charged to the account. If I do not make payments as agreed, the security interest allows Shears to repossess only the merchandise which has not been paid in full.

   _____

   _____

   _____

3. Upon my default, Shears may charge me reasonable attorney's fees. I am responsible for any loss or damage to the merchandise until the price is fully paid.

   _____

   _____

   _____

Warranties

adjustments minor changes or repairs

authorized dealer person licensed or trained to sell and service a particular product

free trial an offer to try a product out before you decide to buy it and accept the terms of the warranty

full warranty a guarantee to service, repair, or replace a product for a specified time at no cost to the purchaser. Damage resulting from careless use will not be covered

guarantee same as a warranty; legal promise

incidental or consequential damages any damages resulting from the owner's carelessness

limited warranty a guarantee to service, repair, or replace a product with the purchaser sharing some of the cost. Warranties usually cover defects in materials and workmanship, not careless use.

maintenance everyday care

manufacturer person who makes a product

prepaid paid in advance; describes freight or postage paid by the buyer

purchaser person who buys a product; consumer

refund give back

repair fix; make work

warranty guarantee; legal promise

workmanship how well something is put together

A warranty is the maker's promise that a product is well made. Warranties usually come with such things as cars, tools, appliances, machinery, and electronic equipment.

Every buyer needs to know how to read a warranty. Study the list of words above. It pays to know these words. You will find them in most warranties.

ACTIVITY 6
Using warranty words

Match the warranty words below with their meanings:

—— 1. repairs   **A.** to mistreat or misuse

—— 2. guarantee   **B.** maker of a product

—— 3. prepaid   **C.** person licensed to sell or service a product

—— 4. abuse   **D.** how well something is put together

—— 5. authorized dealer   **E.** warranty

—— 6. manufacturer   **F.** paid in advance

—— 7. adjustments   **G.** minor changes

—— 8. workmanship   **H.** fixes

ACTIVITY 7
Using warranty words

Use these words to complete the statements below:

limited warranty	prepaid	manufacturer
full warranty	defects	authorized dealer

1. Marion Martin found the address of the ——————————————— on her warranty.

2. Because Bill Peter's stereo was under ———————————, the repairs did not cost him anything.

3. John Anderson has a ——————————— on his stereo and had to pay for some of the parts needed to repair it.

4. All freight charges had to be ——————— when Nancy Ames sent her camera to the nearest service center for repairs.

5. Because there were so many ——————————— in Tommy Thomas's new color TV set, the merchant, an ——————————————————, replaced it.

Reading a warranty

Smart shoppers read the warranties on the products they buy. The warranties tell them (1) the time period during which the manufacturer will repair, replace, or service a product, (2) whether they will have to pay for repairs or services, (3) who made a product, and (4) how to go about having that product repaired or replaced.

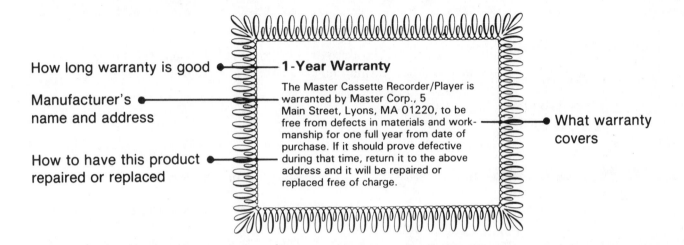

How long warranty is good ●

Manufacturer's ● name and address

How to have this product ● repaired or replaced

1-Year Warranty

The Master Cassette Recorder/Player is warranted by Master Corp., 5 Main Street, Lyons, MA 01220, to be free from defects in materials and workmanship for one full year from date of purchase. If it should prove defective during that time, return it to the above address and it will be repaired or replaced free of charge.

● What warranty covers

ACTIVITY 8
Reading warranties for details

Answer the questions about the warranty below.

1-Year Limited Warranty

This quality Sharp CB equipment is warranted by Sharp Electronics Corp., 10 Keystone Place, Paramus, N.J. 07651, to be free from defects in workmanship and materials for one year from date of purchase. If it proves defective during that time, return it to the above address and it will be repaired or replaced free.

1. What is the name of the product under warranty? _____

_____

2. What are the name and address of the manufacturer?_____

_____

3. What does the warranty cover? _____

_____

4. How long is it good? _____

_____

5. What do you do if this product doesn't work? _____

_____

ACTIVITY 9
Reading warranties for details

Some warranties are more detailed than others. Read the warranty below. Decide whether the statements about it are TRUE (T) or FALSE (F).

AMERICAN PRODUCT CO. FULL FIVE-YEAR WARRANTY

COVERAGE: For five years from the date of original consumer purchase of this product, we promise, without charge, to repair or replace, at our option, any defects in material or workmanship. Warranty coverage does not include defects due to lack of care (see accompanying instruction manual for guidance); and any other warranties made by any other person, including authorized distributors of our products.

ALL INCIDENTAL AND CONSEQUENTIAL DAMAGES ARE EXCLUDED FROM WARRANTY COVERAGE. SOME STATES DO NOT ALLOW THE EXCLUSION OR LIMITATION OF INCIDENTAL OR CONSEQUENTIAL DAMAGES, SO THE ABOVE EXCLUSION MAY NOT APPLY TO YOU. THIS WARRANTY GIVES YOU SPECIFIC LEGAL RIGHTS, AND YOU MAY ALSO HAVE OTHER RIGHTS WHICH VARY FROM STATE TO STATE.

WARRANTY SERVICE PROCEDURE: When warranty service is needed, deliver or send the product insured and properly packaged, freight prepaid, with a description of the apparent defect and the means to ascertain the date of original consumer purchase (such as a copy of your billing or cancelled check) to one of the factory service centers listed below. If, at any time, you are not satisfied with our warranty service, contact: Vice President, Distribution & Service, American Product Co., 2606 W. Water Street, Minneapolis, Minnesota 55408.

USA:
American Product Co.
General Service Department
2606 W. Water Street
Minneapolis, Minnesota 55408

CANADA:
American Product Co.
General Service Department
138 Tannin Road
Toronto, Ontario M4A 1P4

_____ **1.** This is a limited warranty.

_____ **2.** This warranty is good for five years.

_____ **3.** There will be a small charge if your binoculars have to be replaced.

_____ **4.** There will be no charge if your binoculars have to be repaired.

_____ **5.** If you do not take care of your binoculars as described in your manual, they are still under warranty.

_____ **6.** This warranty covers incidental and consequential damages.

_____ **7.** If you send these binoculars in to be serviced, you must pay the shipping charges in advance.

_____ **8.** You do not have to insure the binoculars when you send them.

_____ **9.** You should include something to show the date of purchase when you send this product in for servicing.

_____ **10.** If you're unhappy with the warranty service you receive, you can write the Vice-President of Distribution and Service.

ACTIVITY 10
Reading a car warranty

Every new car owner needs to know how to read a warranty. The warranty explains how to best service and maintain the new car. Car warranties also list what *is* covered and what *is not* covered. Some items will be covered only if a car is properly taken care of. Answer the questions about the following car warranty. The first set of questions deals with what *is* covered. The second set of questions deals with what *is not* covered.

1992 GENERAL MOTORS CORPORATION

General Motors Corporation will provide for repairs to the vehicle during the

WHAT IS COVERED

REPAIRS COVERED
This warranty covers repairs to correct any vehicle defect related to materials or workmanship noted during the WARRANTY PERIOD. New or remanufactured parts will be used.

WARRANTY PERIOD
The WARRANTY PERIOD for all coverages begins on the date the vehicle is first delivered or put in use and ends at the expiration of the BUMPER TO BUMPER PLUS COVERAGE or other COVERAGES shown below.

BUMPER TO BUMPER PLUS COVERAGE
The complete vehicle, (except for additional coverage listed here under "WHAT IS COVERED" and those items listed under "WHAT IS NOT COVERED" on pages 8 and 9) is covered for 3 years or 36,000 miles, whichever comes first.

Some adjustments are covered. See Page 10 "Adjustments", for coverage details.

Maintenance items are covered up to their first scheduled replacement interval only. Also, parts needing replacement, deterioration of paint, trim and appearance items because of ordinary wear from use, are not covered. See "Maintenance" page 9 for details.

BATTERY COVERAGE
If battery replacement is required during the first Year or 12,000 Miles, whichever comes first, from the date of first delivery, it will be free of charge. Replacement after the first Year or 12,000 Miles, but before 3 Years or 36,000 Miles, whichever occurs first, shall be subject to a prorated charge. See page 10 for details.

SUPPLEMENTAL INFLATABLE RESTRAINT COVERAGE (Air Bag)
The Supplemental Inflatable Restraint System (Air Bag) is covered for 3 years, regardless of mileage.

NEW CAR LIMITED WARRANTY

warranty period in accordance with the following terms, conditions and limitations.

CORROSION (RUST-THROUGH) COVERAGE
Any body sheet metal panel that Rusts-Through due to corrosion is covered for 6 Years or 100,000 Miles, whichever comes first. Sheet metal panels may be repaired or replaced. See page 10 for details.

OBTAINING REPAIRS
To obtain warranty repairs, take the car to a Buick dealership within the WARRANTY PERIOD and request the needed repairs. A reasonable time must be allowed for the dealership to perform necessary repairs.

TOWING
TOWING is covered to the nearest Buick dealership, if your vehicle cannot be driven because of a warranted defect.

NO CHARGE
Warranty repairs, including TOWING, parts and labor, will be made at NO CHARGE.

WARRANTY APPLIES
This warranty is for GM cars registered in the United States and normally operated in the United States or Canada, and is provided to the original and any subsequent owners of the car during the WARRANTY PERIOD.

(Cont'd. next page)

What is covered
Write the letter that best completes these statements about this warranty.

_____ 1. General Motors Corporation will provide for repairs to the vehicle
  a. as long as you own it.
  b. during the warranty period, without limitations.
  c. during the warranty period, with certain terms, conditions, and limitations.
  d. for six (6) years.

_____ 2. Repairs will be made by
  a. the General Motors Corporation.
  b. any mechanic you choose.
  c. the Buick dealer where you bought your car.
  d. any Buick dealer.

_____ 3. The warranty period is for
  a. one year (12 months).
  b. three years or 36,000 miles, whichever comes first
  c. one year or 12,000 miles, whichever you choose.
  d. one year or 12,000 miles, whichever comes first.

_____ 4. This warranty begins
  a. when the car is delivered or put into use.
  b. when you pay your deposit on the car.
  c. the date your car is delivered to the dealer.
  d. the date you decide on the car you want.

1992 GENERAL MOTORS CORPORATION

WHAT IS NOT COVERED

TIRES

Tires are warranted separately by the tire maker. See tire warranty folder for details. See page 5 for details.

NOTE: If tire damage is caused by defects in material or workmanship of the vehicle, General Motors will cover the replacement of the tire under the BUMPER TO BUMPER PLUS COVERAGE.

DAMAGE DUE TO ACCIDENT, MISUSE, OR ALTERATION

Damage caused as the result of any of the following, is not covered:
- Collision, fire, theft, freezing, vandalism, riot, explosion or objects striking the vehicle;
- Misuse of the vehicle such as driving over curbs, overloading, racing or other competition. Proper vehicle use is discussed in the Owner's Manual;
- Alteration or modification to the vehicle including the body, chassis or components, after final assembly by General Motors. In addition, coverages do not apply if the odometer mileage cannot be determined because it has been disconnected or the mileage reading has been altered.

DAMAGE OR CORROSION DUE TO ENVIRONMENT, CHEMICAL TREATMENTS OR AFTERMARKET PRODUCTS

Damage caused by airborne fallout (chemicals, tree sap, etc.), stones, hail, earthquake, water or flood, windstorm, lightning, the application of chemicals or sealants subsequent to manufacture, etc., is not covered.

DAMAGE DUE TO LACK OF MAINTENANCE OR USE OF WRONG FUEL, OIL OR LUBRICANTS

Damage caused by failure to follow the requirements of the Maintenance Schedule; failure to follow Maintenance Schedule intervals; and failure to use or maintain proper levels of fluids, fuel, oil and lubricants recommended in the Owner's Manual is not covered. Proper maintenance is the owner's responsibility. GM recommends that you keep all receipts and make them available if questions arise about maintenance.

NEW CAR LIMITED WARRANTY (Cont'd.)

MAINTENANCE

Normal maintenance such as those detailed in the Owner's Manual are not covered and are the owners expense. Examples include:
- Cleaning and polishing
- Lubrication and filters
- Spark plugs
- Windshield wiper blades
- Clutch and brake linings
- Light bulbs

EXTRA EXPENSES

Economic loss or extra expense is not covered. Examples include:
- Loss of vehicle use
- Inconvenience
- Storage
- Payment for loss of time or pay
- Vehicle rental expense
- Lodging, meals or other travel costs

OTHER TERMS: This warranty gives you specific legal rights and you may also have other rights which vary from state to state.

General Motors does not authorize any person to create for it any other obligation or liability in connection with these cars. ANY IMPLIED WARRANTY OF MERCHANTABILITY OR FITNESS FOR A PARTICULAR PURPOSE APPLICABLE TO THIS CAR IS LIMITED IN DURATION TO THE DURATION OF THIS WRITTEN WARRANTY. PERFORMANCE OF REPAIRS AND NEEDED ADJUSTMENTS IS THE EXCLUSIVE REMEDY UNDER THIS WRITTEN WARRANTY OR ANY IMPLIED WARRANTY. GENERAL MOTORS SHALL NOT BE LIABLE FOR INCIDENTAL OR CONSEQUENTIAL DAMAGES SUCH AS, BUT NOT LIMITED TO, LOST WAGES OR VEHICLE RENTAL EXPENSES RESULTING FROM BREACH OF THIS WRITTEN WARRANTY OR ANY IMPLIED WARRANTY.*

* Some states do not allow limitations on how long an implied warranty will last or the exclusion or limitation of incidental or consequential damages, so the above limitations or exclusions may not apply to you.

What is not covered

Answer these questions about this warranty.

1. Give three examples from this warranty of damages due to accidents, misuse, or alterations.

_____

_____

2. Give two examples from this warranty of damages from the environment.

_____

_____

3. Who pays for routine maintenance services?

_____

4. How can you determine *when* your new car needs maintenance?

_____

_____

Choose the best answer to complete the following statements

_____ 1. "Incidental or consequential" damages describe
   a. defects in workmanship.
   b. defects in the materials.
   c. damage from careless use.

_____ 2. When you send a defective product back to the manufacturer for a repair,
   a. you usually pay the postage.
   b. the manufacturer will pay the postage.
   c. the store where you bought it will pay the postage.

_____ 3. "Damages resulting from workmanship" means
   a. you damaged it when you put it together.
   b. the product was not put together correctly at the factory.
   c. the product was incorrectly packed.

_____ 4. The digital watch you purchased stopped working within one month of purchase. It is covered by a one-year warranty. You should
   a. send or take the watch to the place where you bought it.
   b. take the watch to a local jeweler for repair.
   c. read the warranty and send or take the watch to the place specified.

_____ 5. The warranty on a new car begins
   a. when you order the car.
   b. ten days after you get the car.
   c. when the car is delivered to you.

_____ 6. The tires on new cars are
   a. warranted by the tire maker.
   b. warranted by the automobile company.
   c. not covered by any warranty.

_____ 7. If you buy a new car in New York, and it breaks down in California during the warranty period,
   a. you can take it to an authorized dealer in California.
   b. you must pay for repairs because only the dealer who sold it to you will fix it without charge.
   c. you must pay for repairs and send the bill to the dealer in New York.

_____ 8. If your car windshield is broken by a tree limb during a high wind and the car is under warranty,
   a. the car dealer will replace the windshield without charge.
   b. the car dealer will charge to replace the windshield.
   c. you will pay one-half of the cost of replacing the windshield.

_____ 9. An authorized dealer is
   a. anyone who sells the product.
   b. a seller who is licensed by the manufacturer to sell and service the product.
   c. a repair service.

_____ 10. Warranties usually cover
   a. any damage to a product during the time of the warranty.
   b. defects in workmanship and materials during the time of the warranty.
   c. defects in the product caused by heat or extreme cold.

SHOW WHAT YOU KNOW . . .

About Warranties

Write a warranty for a product you create. Include the necessary parts of a warranty. You determine if it will be a full or limited warranty.

Reference strategies

Do you know how to use a computer or a card catalog to find a book in a library? Do you know how useful a dictionary is? Do you use a book's index or table of contents when you need information quickly?

In this chapter you will learn about using the library. You will also practice dictionary skills and learn how to use tables of contents and indexes. All of these are reference skills. The first topic is using the library.

The library

WORDS TO KNOW

alphabetical   in the same order as the letters of the alphabet

call number   set of numbers and letters used by a library to identify a book

call slip   a form for writing down the author, title, and call number of a book

card catalog   a collection of cards in drawers that lists the books in a library

circulation desk   the place in a library where books are checked in and out

closed shelves   parts of a library not open to users

cross reference   the suggestion of an additional source to examine

Dewey decimal system   a system of classifying books by subjects

encyclopedia   a book or set of books that has articles on many subjects

fiction   writing, such as novels and short stories, that tell about imaginary people and happenings

general collection   the materials in a library that can be checked out

nonfiction   writing, such as history and biography, that deals with real people or events

numerical order   in order by numbers

periodical   something published weekly or monthly like a magazine

reference book   a book, such as a dictionary or an encyclopedia, used to find facts or information quickly

A library has three kinds of resources. One is the general collection. You may check out books from this group. A card catalog or computer helps you find these books. To search for books you must understand the Dewey decimal system. Another resource is the reference collection. It has dictionaries, encyclopedias, and more. You must use these books at the library. The third kind of resource is periodicals. The periodicals collection has pamphlets and magazines. You must also use these at the library.

The card catalog

Some libraries have a card catalog. It helps readers find the books they want.

All books in the library are listed in the card catalog. The card catalog helps identify and locate books. It is a series of drawers. The cards in each drawer are arranged alphabetically. The drawers are also arranged alphabetically. Each drawer has cards listing books in the library. You can find a book listed in the catalog by *author, title,* or *subject.*

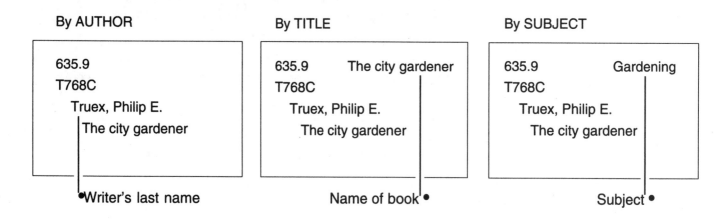

How do you find a book you want? There are several ways. You can look up the author's last name. You can look up the title of the book. Or you can look up the subject you want to read about. Author and title cards are often in one section of the card catalog. Subject cards are in their own section.

When you find the card, you must note the call number from the card.

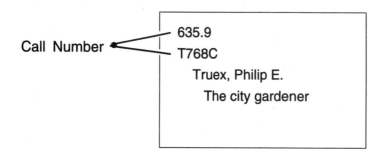

The call number on the author, title, and subject cards is the same. It is in the upper left-hand corner. This call number directs you to the book. Call numbers are based on the Dewey decimal system of subject categories. See pages 223–224 for more information about the Dewey decimal system. *The City Gardener* by Philip Truex has call number 635.9 T768C. This tells you that it is in the 600 section of the library. All the books are on the shelves in numerical order. You locate the books in the 600 section of the library. Then you find the books marked 635. The *T* stands for the first letter of the author's last name. Your book should be among these. Works of fiction are put on the shelves alphabetically by the author's last name. They will be in a section of the library labeled "Fiction." Many libraries also have separate sections labeled "Poetry" and "Drama."

Here are things to keep in mind when you are searching for a book in a card catalog.

- Look for authors by their last name. For example, look for Alice Walker under Walker.

- Subject cards show last names first, too. If your subject is Eleanor Roosevelt, look under her last name in the card file.

- Ignore *a, an,* or *the* if it is the first word in a subject or title. The book title *The Scarlet Letter* will be in the card catalog under *S*.

- Remember there are three ways to find a book. The book *Outline of History* by H. G. Wells can be found by searching for

  the title: *Outline of History*
  the author: Wells, H. G.
  the subject: History.

ACTIVITY 1
Using the card catalog

You want to look up the following authors, titles, and subjects. Look at the drawing of the fronts of the drawers in a library card catalog. Which drawers will have cards on the information you want?

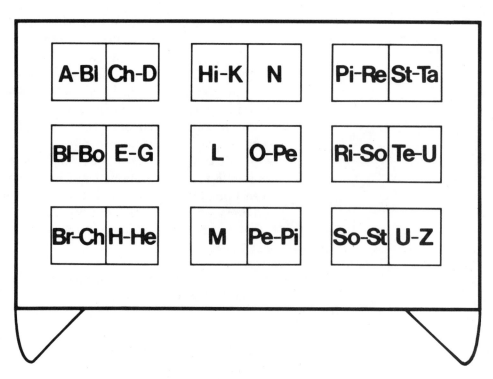

Drawers

1. camping _____

2. *The Outsiders* _____

3. wrestling _____

4. Arna Bontemps _____

5. *The Pearl* _____

6. George Bernard Shaw _____

7. Sandra Cisneros _____

8. *Are You in the House Alone?* _____

9. *A Separate Peace* _____

10. photography _____

11. Toronto _____

12. cooking _____

13. Madeleine L'Engle _____

14. genealogy _____

15. Norma Fox Mazer _____

The computer
Many libraries use computers to store information about their books. Library computer systems are similar, but there are some differences. Each library has detailed instructions on how to use its computer system. In most systems you can find a book by typing in the author, the title, or the subject. You can find out how many books the library has by one author. You can discover the location of the book in the library, and you can tell whether the book is in the library or has been checked out.

Hal's library has a computer system. He wants to find *The City Gardener*, but he can't remember the author. He doesn't know the call number. He won't be able to find the book on the shelves without knowing the call number. Hal will have to look for the book by typing the title into the computer. Here is what he types:

T City Gardener

The *T* stands for *title*. In some systems you must leave a space between *T* and the title. In other systems you must type slash (/) or another symbol after the *T* and before you type the title. After you type the information you want, you must touch a key that starts the search. Sometimes this key is labeled *Enter*. Sometimes it is labeled *Return*.

Here is what Hal sees on the screen after he presses the *Return* key:

NUMBER OF MATCHES: 2

T CITY GARDENER

Choose line number(s) and press return key:

1. CITY GARDENER
2. CITY GARDENERS HANDBOOK FROM BALCONY TO BACKYARD

Hal knows he doesn't want the second title. He wants the first one. He types the number 1 and presses the *Return* key. Here is what he sees next.

Truex, Philip E.
The city gardener

                New York, Knopf [distributed by Random]

	COPIES IN BRANCH: 1		SYSTEM: 7
LOCATION	CALL NUMBER	DUE DATE	STATUS
BST OPEN	635.9T768C	4-04-94	CHARGED

Now Hal knows the author and location. In Hal's library, BST stands for "Business, Science, and Technology." Hal will find the book in this section. Hal also knows the call number. Unfortunately, the book is charged out and is not due until April 4. The computer also shows that Hal's branch of the library has 1 copy. There are 7 copies in the whole system.

Rose wants to find a book by Alice Walker, but she can't remember the title. Here is what she types into the computer. (The *A* stands for author.)

A Alice Walker

Rose has made a mistake. She should have typed the last name first. She sees the following message on the computer screen:

No match found. Try again.

When Rose tries again and types in A Walker Alice, here is what she sees on the screen:

NUMBER OF CITATIONS: 4
A   WALKER ALICE

Choose a line number and press return key:

1. Walker, Alice, 1944–
   The color purple
2. Walker, Alice, 1944–
   Horses make a landscape look more beautiful: poems
3. Walker, Alice, 1944–
   In love and trouble; stories of black women
4. Walker, Alice, 1944–
   In search of our mother's gardens

When Rose sees the first title, *The Color Purple,* she remembers that this is the title she wants. Rose types in the number 1 and presses the *Return* key. The screen then shows this:

Walker, Alice, 1944–
The color purple: a novel

New York, Harcourt Brace Jovanovich

CALL NO.   DUE DATE   STATUS
Fiction W   SHELF

Notice that Alice Walker's birth year is shown. This helps to identify her, since there may be other authors named Alice Walker. Notice also that the city where the book was published is shown. The publisher is also shown. Some systems will also show the date the book was published. Rose will find this book in the Fiction section of the library with the Ws.

If Rose wants to find a book on a particular subject, like carpentry or gymnastics, a librarian can show Rose how to narrow her search. To find gymnastics, for example, she may have to type in Sports—gymnastics.

ACTIVITY 2
Using a computer

Suppose you want to find the following books on a computer. Write the first word of each title that you would type into a computer. Write the part of the author's name that you would type first into the computer. (Titles are in italic type.)

1. *The Witch of Blackbird Pond* _____

2. *Jane Eyre* _____

3. Emily Brontë _____

4. Jane Austen _____

5. *The Old Man and the Sea* _____

6. Arthur Conan Doyle _____

7. M. E. Kerr _____

8. Neil Simon _____

9. *A Raisin in the Sun* _____

10. *David Copperfield* _____

Open and closed shelves

In most libraries you may take a book from a shelf yourself. This is called the *open-shelf system*. You get the book and take it to the checkout desk. You then use your library card to check out the book. Sometimes someone who works at the library gets your book from the shelves. This is called the *closed-shelf system*. Many college and reference libraries have closed shelves. If you use this type of library, you will have to fill out a call slip. This call slip will identify the book you want.

```
┌─────────────────────────────────────────────────────────────┐
│  CALL                                                    CF   │
│  NUMBER      AUTHOR                                       RS   │
│                                                          FS   │
│                                                          PS   │
│              TITLE                                       RE   │
│                                                          IU   │
│                                                          RN   │
│  VOLUME                                                       │
│                                                              │
│              THE · NEWBERRY · LIBRARY                        │
│  NAME                                    DESK                 │
│                                          NUMBER              │
│  ADDRESS                                                     │
│  SCHOOL OR COLLEGE                                           │
└─────────────────────────────────────────────────────────────┘
```

You take your call slip to a call desk. A library employee will get your book using the information you put on the slip. A library with open shelves may have some books that need a call slip. These might be rare or valuable books that need special care and cannot be checked out.

The Dewey decimal system

Libraries are divided into sections. Books on similar subjects are grouped together. This grouping is called the Dewey decimal system. The call number on a book stands for the subject and helps locate the book. Here are the number categories in the Dewey decimal system:

000–099	General works	500–599	Pure sciences
100–199	Philosophy	600–699	Technology
200–299	Religion	700–799	The Arts
300–399	Social sciences	800–899	Literature
400–499	Language	900–999	Geography & History

Each section is further divided into *ten* parts. Here are the ten parts of the 800—Literature:

800	General literature
810	American literature
820	English literature
830	Germanic literature
840	Romance literature
850	Italian, Romanian literature
860	Spanish, Portuguese literature
870	Latin & Italic literature
880	Greek literature
890	Other literatures

Each of these divisions is further divided. Here are the parts of the 820s—English literature:

821	English poetry	826	English letters
822	English drama	827	English satire
823	English fiction	828	English miscellany
824	English essays	829	Anglo-Saxon
825	English oratory		

Any further divisions are shown with a decimal. For example, a call number might be 821.09.

Some large libraries do not use the Dewey decimal system. They use the Library of Congress system. Both systems have author, title, and subject cards. Both systems use call numbers, but the Library of Congress system divides books into lettered classes:

A	General works
B	Philosophy—Religion
C	History—Auxiliary Sciences
D	History and Topography (except America)
E-F	America
G	Geography—Anthropology
H	Social Sciences (Economics and Sociology)
J	Political Science
K	Law
L	Education
M	Music
N	Fine Arts
P	Language and Literature
Q	Science
R	Medicine
S	Agriculture
T	Technology
U	Military Science
V	Naval Science
Z	Bibliography and Library Science

ACTIVITY 3
Using the Dewey decimal system

Rose and Hal are browsing through the library. They each have a list of topics they would like to know more about. In which section of the library would each of them go to find books on the topics below? Use the Dewey decimal numbers to show the sections.

000–099	General works	500–599	Pure sciences
100–199	Philosophy	600–699	Technology
200–299	Religion	700–799	The Arts
300–399	Social sciences	800–899	Literature
400–499	Language	900–999	Geography & History

Rose's List

1. American literature ─────────────

2. Oriental philosophy ─────────────

3. English poets ─────────────

4. Women artists ─────────────

5. Botany ─────────────

Hal's List

6. Chemistry ─────────────

7. African history ─────────────

8. Building construction ─────────────

9. The Bible ─────────────

10. slang ─────────────

The Readers' Guide to Periodical Literature

Suppose you want to find something in a back issue of a magazine. Magazines are not shown in a card catalog. You will need to use the *Readers' Guide to Periodical Literature*. This reference work has many volumes. It will help you find what you want in a magazine.

In the front of the *Readers' Guide* is a list of the magazines that are in the guide. Here are some of the magazines.

American Craft	*Down Beat*
American Heritage	*Ebony*
Better Homes and Gardens	*Motor Trend*
Black Enterprise	*National Wildlife*
Car and Driver	*Popular Mechanics*
Consumer Reports	*Popular Science*
Cycle	*Rolling Stone*
Dance Magazine	*Runner's World*

Here are some of the abbreviations used in the entries in the *Readers' Guide.*

J	January	+	continued on later pages
F	February		of same issue
Mr	March	por	portrait
Ap	April	int	interviewer
My	May	m	monthly
Je	June	pt	part
Jl	July	v	volume
Ag	August	w	weekly
S	September	il	illustrated
O	October		
N	November		
D	December		

Here is a sample entry from the March 1980–February 1981 *Readers' Guide.*

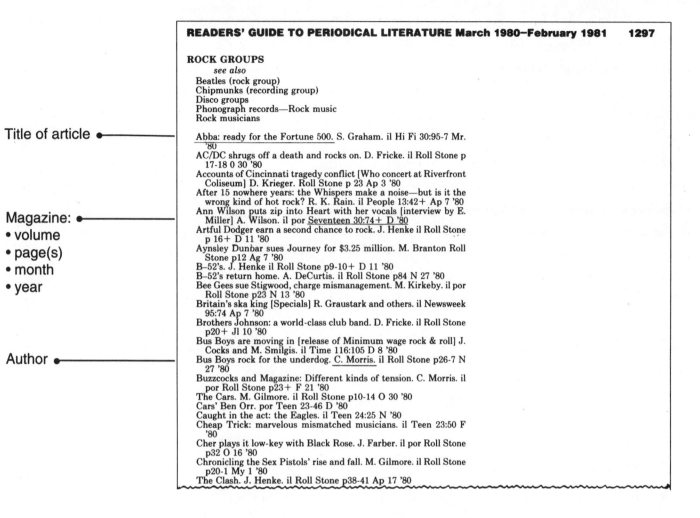

Title of article

Magazine:
• volume
• page(s)
• month
• year

Author

READERS' GUIDE TO PERIODICAL LITERATURE March 1980–February 1981   1297

ROCK GROUPS
    see also
Beatles (rock group)
Chipmunks (recording group)
Disco groups
Phonograph records—Rock music
Rock musicians

Abba: ready for the Fortune 500. S. Graham. il Hi Fi 30:95-7 Mr.
    '80
AC/DC shrugs off a death and rocks on. D. Fricke. il Roll Stone p
    17-18 O 30 '80
Accounts of Cincinnati tragedy conflict [Who concert at Riverfront
    Coliseum] D. Krieger. Roll Stone p 23 Ap 3 '80
After 15 nowhere years: the Whispers make a noise—but is it the
    wrong kind of hot rock? R. K. Rain. il People 13:42+ Ap 7 '80
Ann Wilson puts zip into Heart with her vocals [interview by E.
    Miller] A. Wilson. il por Seventeen 30:74+ D '80
Artful Dodger earn a second chance to rock. J. Henke il Roll Stone
    p 16+ D 11 '80
Aynsley Dunbar sues Journey for $3.25 million. M. Branton Roll
    Stone p12 Ag 7 '80
B–52's. J. Henke il Roll Stone p9-10+ D 11 '80
B–52's return home. A. DeCurtis. il Roll Stone p84 N 27 '80
Bee Gees sue Stigwood, charge mismanagement. M. Kirkeby. il por
    Roll Stone p23 N 13 '80
Britain's ska king [Specials] R. Graustark and others. il Newsweek
    95:74 Ap 7 '80
Brothers Johnson: a world-class club band. D. Fricke. il Roll Stone
    p20+ Jl 10 '80
Bus Boys are moving in [release of Minimum wage rock & roll] J.
    Cocks and M. Smilgis. il Time 116:105 D 8 '80
Bus Boys rock for the underdog. C. Morris. il Roll Stone p26-7 N
    27 '80
Buzzcocks and Magazine: Different kinds of tension. C. Morris. il
    por Roll Stone p23+ F 21 '80
The Cars. M. Gilmore. il Roll Stone p10-14 O 30 '80
Cars' Ben Orr. por Teen 23-46 D '80
Caught in the act: the Eagles. il Teen 24:25 N '80
Cheap Trick: marvelous mismatched musicians. il Teen 23:50 F
    '80
Cher plays it low-key with Black Rose. J. Farber. il por Roll Stone
    p32 O 16 '80
Chronicling the Sex Pistols' rise and fall. M. Gilmore. il Roll Stone
    p20-1 My 1 '80
The Clash. J. Henke. il Roll Stone p38-41 Ap 17 '80

The subject head is "Rock groups." Subject heads are either topics or
authors' names. They are alphabetical. Entries are alphabetical by title.
When you find what you are looking for in the *Readers' Guide*, you will need
to go to the periodicals section of a library. Here you will find bound back
issues of many magazines. If you wanted to read the article on Abba, you
would look for the March 1980 issue of *Hi Fi* magazine.

ACTIVITY 4
Using the Readers' Guide

Study the sample entries from the *Readers' Guide to Periodical Literature.* Answer the following questions.

1. Cross references are shown under the subject head. A reader looking up rock groups could also look under other subject heads. What are two other subject heads that would have information on rock groups?

   _____

2. What is the title of the first article?

   _____

3. In what magazine did the first article appear? _____

4. Where would you find an article about Cheap Trick? _____

5. "Bus Boys rock for the underdog" is the title of an article in what issue of *Rolling Stone?*

   _____

6. What would you look under to find all the articles on the Chipmunks?

   _____

7. Who wrote about Cher? _____ Is the article illustrated? _____

8. Articles about the B–52's appeared in which two months of *Rolling Stone* in 1980?

   _____

9. Look at the entry for "After 15 nowhere years." What is the volume number of the *People* in which it appears? _____

10. Was Ann Wilson a singer in 1980?

    _____

The statements below are about the library. Mark these statements TRUE (T) or FALSE (F).

_____ **1.** To find an author in a card catalog, you must look under the last name.

_____ **2.** To find an author in a computerized catalog, you must look under the last name.

_____ **3.** A library computer will show you the call number of a book.

_____ **4.** A library computer may tell you whether a book is checked out or on the shelf.

_____ **5.** You can find books by subject in the card catalog and on a computer.

_____ **6.** The Dewey decimal system is a reference work in the general collection.

_____ **7.** A call slip is used to obtain a book in a library that has open shelves.

_____ **8.** In some libraries, books are arranged according to the Library of Congress system.

_____ **9.** If a book title begins with *Of,* you must search for the book under the second word in the title.

_____ **10.** The *Readers' Guide to Periodical Literature* will be in the fiction section of the library.

SHOW WHAT YOU KNOW . . .

About Reference Works

Find *one* fascinating fact in one of the following reference works and report it to the class: almanac, gazetteer, world atlas.

Dictionary skills

accent   special emphasis given to a syllable in pronouncing a word

antonym   a word opposite in meaning to another word, for example, *good* and *bad* are antonyms

entry or entry word   word that is explained in a dictionary

etymology   the origin or source of a word

guide word   word at the top of a page that lets you know what part of the alphabet is on that page

homograph   word having the same spelling as another word but a different meaning and origin. *Bow,* a tie, and *bow,* to bend, are homographs.

homophone   word having the same pronunciation as another word but a different meaning and origin. *Bow,* to bend, and *bough,* a tree branch, are homophones.

illustrative sentence   sentence in a definition that shows how a word is used

part of speech   a label that tells how a word is used in a sentence. A *noun* (word that names something) is one of the eight parts of speech.

pronunciation key   chart showing how to pronounce words

restrictive label   label that indicates a word is not part of the standard vocabulary of all speakers

schwa   unstressed vowel sound, such as the *i* in *pencil;* the symbol for a schwa is ə.

syllable   word or part of a word pronounced as a unit

synonym   a word with the same or nearly the same meaning as another word; *little* and *small* are synonyms.

usage note   note after a definition that tells how words are used

---

A dictionary is an important reference work. All the words in a dictionary are in one alphabetical list. This list makes up the main part of a dictionary. Many dictionaries have special sections at the back. These sections may have maps, pictures of state or national flags, listings of state capitals, or other lists of facts. You can find a lot of information if you know how to use a dictionary.

Types of dictionaries

Dictionaries are not all the same. Some dictionaries are intended for use by young children. Some are intended for high school or college students. There are paperbound dictionaries, which have smaller type and fewer entries than most high school or college dictionaries. Large dictionaries, called *unabridged dictionaries,* are not portable and have many more words than college dictionaries. Many people and all libraries have unabridged dictionaries.

Ways of defining and pronouncing words can be different in various dictionaries. Some dictionaries place an accent mark before a syllable and others place it after. The symbols used to show pronunciation may mean different things in different dictionaries. Some dictionaries have a few drawings to help you understand definitions. Others have many drawings and photos. Sometimes biographical and geographical names are at the back of a dictionary and sometimes they are included in the regular alphabetical listing as in the following example from a page of *Webster's Ninth New Collegiate Dictionary:*

> **geo·pol·i·tics** \-'päl-ə-,tiks\ *n pl but sing in constr* (1904) **1** : a study of the influence of such factors as geography, economics, and demography on the politics and esp. the foreign policy of a state **2** : a governmental policy guided by geopolitics **3** : a combination of political and geographic factors relating to something (as a state or particular resources) — **geo·po·lit·i·cal** \-pə-'lit-i-kəl\ *adj* — **geo·po·lit·i·cal·ly** \-i-k(ə-)lē\ *adv*
> **geo·pres·sured** \,jē-ō-'presh-ərd\ *adj* (1968) : subjected to great pressure from geologic forces (~ methane)
> **Geor·die** \'jȯrd-ē\ *n* [Sc. dim. of the name *George*] *chiefly Brit* (1866) : an inhabitant of Newcastle-upon-Tyre or its environs; *also* : the dialect of English spoken by Geordies
> **George** \'jȯ(ə)rj\ *n* [St. *George*] (1506) **1** : either of two of the insignia of the British Order of the Garter **2** : a British coin bearing the image of St. George
> **geor·gette** \jȯr-'jet\ *n* [fr. *Georgette,* a trademark] (1915) : a thin strong clothing crepe of fibers woven from hard-twisted yarns to produce a dull pebbly surface
> **¹Geor·gian** \'jȯr-jən\ *n* (15c) **1** : a native or inhabitant of Georgia in the Caucasus **2** : the language of the Georgian people
> **²Georgian** *adj* (1607) : of, relating to, or constituting Georgia in the Caucasus, the Georgians, or Georgian
> **³Georgian** *n* (1741) : a native or resident of the state of Georgia
> **⁴Georgian** *adj* (1762) : of, relating to, or characteristic of the state of Georgia or its people
> **⁵Georgian** *adj* (1875) **1** : of, relating to, or characteristic of the reigns of the first four Georges of Great Britain **2** : of, relating to, or characteristic of the reign of George V of Great Britain
> **⁶Georgian** *n* (1901) **1** : one belonging to either of the Georgian periods **2** : Georgian taste or style
> **Geor·gia pine** \,jȯr-jə-\ *n* (1796) : LONGLEAF PINE
> **¹geor·gic** \'jȯr-jik\ *n* [the *Georgics,* poem by Vergil, fr. L *georgicus*] (1513) : a poem dealing with agriculture

It is a good idea to own an up-to-date school or college dictionary. You should become thoroughly familiar with your dictionary so that you can use it easily. The more you use one dictionary, the easier it will be to understand all its features.

ACTIVITY 5
Locating words in a dictionary

The words below are entries from a dictionary. These words are no longer in alphabetical order. Arrange these words alphabetically.

Dictionary entries	Alphabetical arrangement	Dictionary entries	Alphabetical arrangement
complex	_____	possessed	_____
competitive	_____	possess	_____
complacency	_____	posse	_____
complacence	_____	position	_____
compete	_____	point	_____
competency	_____	postage	_____

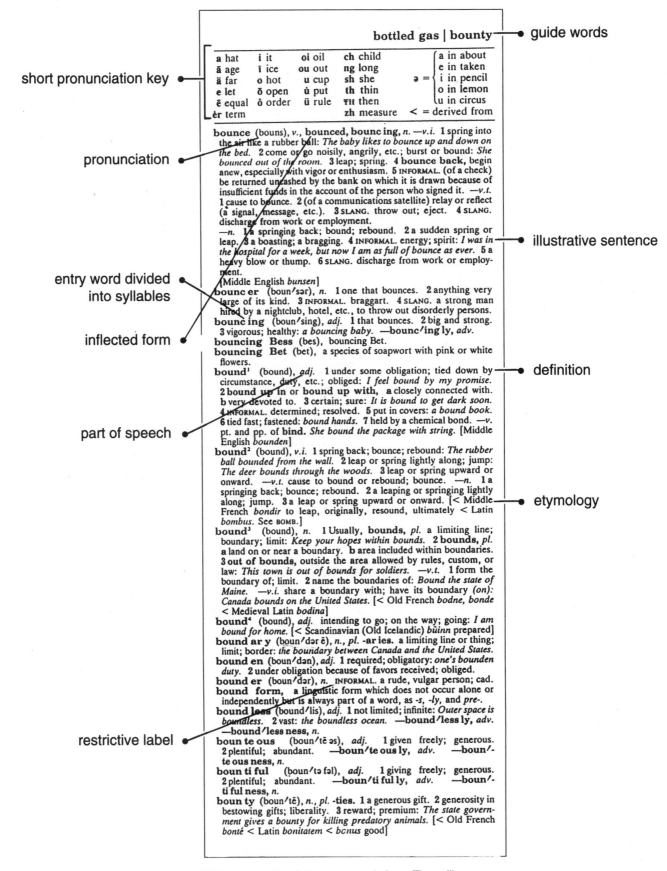

short pronunciation key

pronunciation

entry word divided into syllables

inflected form

part of speech

restrictive label

guide words

a hat	i it	oi oil	ch child	(a in about
ā age	ī ice	ou out	ng long		e in taken
ä far	o hot	u cup	sh she	ə = { i in pencil
e let	ō open	u̇ put	th thin		o in lemon
ē equal	ô order	ü rule	ŦH then	(u in circus
ėr term			zh measure	< = derived from

bounce (bouns), *v.*, **bounced, bounc ing,** *n.* —*v.i.* **1** spring into the air like a rubber ball: *The baby likes to bounce up and down on the bed.* **2** come or go noisily, angrily, etc.; burst or bound: *She bounced out of the room.* **3** leap; spring. **4 bounce back,** begin anew, especially with vigor or enthusiasm. **5** INFORMAL. (of a check) be returned uncashed by the bank on which it is drawn because of insufficient funds in the account of the person who signed it. —*v.t.* **1** cause to bounce. **2** (of a communications satellite) relay or reflect (a signal, message, etc.). **3** SLANG. throw out; eject. **4** SLANG. discharge from work or employment.
—*n.* **1** a springing back; bound; rebound. **2** a sudden spring or leap. **3** a boasting; a bragging. **4** INFORMAL. energy; spirit: *I was in the hospital for a week, but now I am as full of bounce as ever.* **5** a heavy blow or thump. **6** SLANG. discharge from work or employment.
[Middle English *bunsen*]

bounc er (boun′sər), *n.* **1** one that bounces. **2** anything very large of its kind. **3** INFORMAL. braggart. **4** SLANG. a strong man hired by a nightclub, hotel, etc., to throw out disorderly persons.

bounc ing (boun′sing), *adj.* **1** that bounces. **2** big and strong. **3** vigorous; healthy: *a bouncing baby.* —**bounc′ing ly,** *adv.*

bouncing Bess (bes), bouncing Bet.

bouncing Bet (bet), a species of soapwort with pink or white flowers.

bound¹ (bound), *adj.* **1** under some obligation; tied down by circumstance, duty, etc.; obliged: *I feel bound by my promise.* **2 bound up in** or **bound up with,** a closely connected with. **b** very devoted to. **3** certain; sure: *It is bound to get dark soon.* **4** INFORMAL. determined; resolved. **5** put in covers: *a bound book.* **6** tied fast; fastened: *bound hands.* **7** held by a chemical bond. —*v.* pt. and pp. of **bind.** *She bound the package with string.* [Middle English *bounden*]

bound² (bound), *v.i.* **1** spring back; bounce; rebound: *The rubber ball bounded from the wall.* **2** leap or spring lightly along; jump: *The deer bounds through the woods.* **3** leap or spring upward or onward. —*v.t.* cause to bound or rebound; bounce. —*n.* **1** a springing back; bounce; rebound. **2** a leaping or springing lightly along; jump. **3** a leap or spring upward or onward. [< Middle French *bondir* to leap, originally, resound, ultimately < Latin *bombus.* See BOMB.]

bound³ (bound), *n.* **1** Usually, **bounds,** *pl.* a limiting line; boundary; limit: *Keep your hopes within bounds.* **2 bounds,** *pl.* **a** land on or near a boundary. **b** area included within boundaries. **3 out of bounds,** outside the area allowed by rules, custom, or law: *This town is out of bounds for soldiers.* —*v.t.* **1** form the boundary of; limit. **2** name the boundaries of: *Bound the state of Maine.* —*v.i.* share a boundary with; have its boundary *(on)*: *Canada bounds on the United States.* [< Old French *bodne, bonde* < Medieval Latin *bodina*]

bound⁴ (bound), *adj.* intending to go; on the way; going: *I am bound for home.* [< Scandinavian (Old Icelandic) *búinn* prepared]

bound ar y (boun′dər ē), *n.*, *pl.* **-ar ies.** a limiting line or thing; limit; border: *the boundary between Canada and the United States.*

bound en (boun′dən), *adj.* **1** required; obligatory: *one's bounden duty.* **2** under obligation because of favors received; obliged.

bound er (boun′dər), *n.* INFORMAL. a rude, vulgar person; cad.

bound form, a linguistic form which does not occur alone or independently but is always part of a word, as *-s, -ly,* and *pre-.*

bound less (bound′lis), *adj.* **1** not limited; infinite: *Outer space is boundless.* **2** vast: *the boundless ocean.* —**bound′less ly,** *adv.* —**bound′less ness,** *n.*

boun te ous (boun′tē əs), *adj.* **1** given freely; generous. **2** plentiful; abundant. —**boun′te ous ly,** *adv.* —**boun′te ous ness,** *n.*

boun ti ful (boun′tə fəl), *adj.* **1** giving freely; generous. **2** plentiful; abundant. —**boun′ti ful ly,** *adv.* —**boun′ti ful ness,** *n.*

boun ty (boun′tē), *n.*, *pl.* **-ties. 1** a generous gift. **2** generosity in bestowing gifts; liberality. **3** reward; premium: *The state government gives a bounty for killing predatory animals.* [< Old French *bonté* < Latin *bonitatem* < *bonus* good]

illustrative sentence

definition

etymology

This excerpt of a dictionary page is from *Thorndike Barnhart Advanced Dictionary.*

58

Guide words Guide words can help you locate a word on a dictionary page. Guide words are usually at the top of a page. If there are two guide words at the top of a page, they show the first and last words on that page. (See the illustration on page 58.) Sometimes there is a guide word at the top of the left-hand page and a guide word at the top of the right-hand page. The left guide word shows the first word at the top of the left page. The right guide word shows the last word at the bottom of the right page. You decide whether the word you want falls alphabetically between the guide words.

ACTIVITY 6
Using guide words

Below is a list of words from three different pages of a dictionary. Then there are guide words from those pages. Put each word in the column where it belongs.

history	hogwash	hives
homework	hoax	hint
honey	honest	homage
horoscope	hole	horror
hostage	hotshot	hospital

hilt/hold   **holder/hooky**   **hooligan/houseboat**

_____   _____   _____

_____   _____   _____

_____   _____   _____

_____   _____   _____

_____   _____   _____

Entry words Each word that is explained in a dictionary is called an *entry word*. Entry words are shown divided into syllables.

o pin ion

pub lic

Entries that have two or more words are not usually divided into syllables.

public opinion

public schools

Some two-word entries are divided into syllables, however.

Puer to Ri co

Pronunciation key Dictionaries tell you how to pronounce a word. To pronounce a word you need to learn the pronunciation key. The *symbols* in the key tell you how letters are pronounced. Each symbol stands for a particular sound. A short form of a pronunciation key is usually found on every other dictionary page.

The *schwa* (ə) is one of the symbols used to help you pronounce words correctly. The pronunciation key tells you what a letter or letters sound like when the schwa symbol is used. The following key is from *Thorndike Barnhart Advanced Dictionary*.

Pronunciation Key

a	hat, cap	j	jam, enjoy	u	cup, butter	**foreign sounds**
ā	age, face	k	kind, seek	u̇	full, put	
ä	father, far	l	land, coal	ü	rule, move	Y as in French *du*.
		m	me, am			Pronounce (ē) with the lips
b	bad, rob	n	no, in	v	very, save	rounded as for (ü).
ch	child, much	ng	long, bring	w	will, woman	
d	did, red			y	young, yet	à as in French *ami*.
		o	hot, rock	z	zero, breeze	Pronounce (ä) with the lips
e	let, best	ō	open, go	zh	measure, seizure	spread and held tense.
ē	equal, be	ô	order, all			
ėr	term, learn	oi	oil, voice	ə	represents:	œ as in French *peu*.
		ou	house, out		a in about	Pronounce (ā) with the lips
f	fat, if				e in taken	rounded as for (ô).
g	go, bag	p	paper, cup		i in pencil	
h	he, how	r	run, try		o in lemon	N as in French *bon*.
		s	say, yes		u in circus	The N is not pronounced,
i	it, pin	sh	she, rush			but shows that the vowel
ī	ice, five	t	tell, it			before it is nasal.
		th	thin, both			
		ᴛʜ	then, smooth			H as in German *ach*.
						Pronounce (k) without
						closing the breath passage.

Grammatical Key

adj.	adjective	*prep.*	preposition
adv.	adverb	*pron.*	pronoun
conj.	conjunction	*v.*	verb
interj.	interjection	*v.i.*	intransitive verb
n.	noun	*v.t.*	transitive verb
sing.	singular	*pl.*	plural
pt.	past tense	*pp.*	past participle

ACTIVITY 7
Using the pronunciation key

Using the short pronunciation key, write a word that has the same sound as the symbol in dark type. The first two are done for you.

a hat	**i** it	**oi** oil	**ch** child	⎧ a in about
ā age	**ī** ice	**ou** out	**ng** long	⎪ e in taken
ä far	**o** hot	**u** cup	**sh** she	**ə** = ⎨ i in pencil
e let	**ō** open	**ú** put	**th** thin	⎪ o in lemon
ē equal	**ô** order	**ü** rule	**ŦH** then	⎩ u in circus
ėr term			**zh** measure	**<** = derived from

1. **a** hat _____sat_____
2. **ā** age _____page_____
3. **ä** far _____
4. **e** let _____
5. **ē** equal _____
6. **ėr** term _____
7. **i** it _____
8. **ī** ice _____
9. **o** hot _____
10. **ō** open _____
11. **ô** order _____

12. **oi** oil _____
13. **ou** out _____
14. **u** cup _____
15. **ú** put _____
16. **ü** rule _____
17. **ch** child _____
18. **ng** long _____
19. **sh** she _____
20. **th** thin _____
21. **TH** then _____
22. **zh** measure _____

Accent marks   Pronounce this word with the help of the pronunciation key.

jim nā´ že em

Notice that there is an accent mark after the second syllable. This tells you to stress that syllable. This mark is a *primary accent.* Some words have more than one accent. If a word has a *secondary accent,* the accent mark is in lighter type. Here is a word with two accents. Pronounce the word.

ke les´ te rol

Some words have two or more pronunciations. In some dictionaries the first pronunciation is the one most commonly used.

ACTIVITY 8
Using the pronunciation key and accent marks

Using the pronunciation key, match the pronunciations in Column A with the words in Column B.

a hat	**i** it	**oi** oil	**ch** child	⎧ a in about
ā age	**ī** ice	**ou** out	**ng** long	⎪ e in taken
ä far	**o** hot	**u** cup	**sh** she	ə = ⎨ i in pencil
e let	**ō** open	**u̇** put	**th** thin	⎪ o in lemon
ē equal	**ô** order	**ü** rule	**ᴛʜ** then	⎩ u in circus
ėr term			**zh** measure	**<** = derived from

A   **B**

1. sin´ e me —————————————————   jaw

2. klas´ e kel —————————————————   Florida

3. kom´ ple ka´ shen ——————————————   cinema

4. en s̄i´ kle pē´ dē e ——————————————   joy

5. flôr´ e de —————————————————   classical

6. hyü´ sten —————————————————   encyclopedia

7. jô —————————————————————   complication

8. joi —————————————————————   Houston

9. bī ling´ gwel ——————————————————   thyme

10. tīm —————————————————————   bilingual

11. ᴛʜō —————————————————————   whim

12. hwim —————————————————————   though

SHOW WHAT YOU KNOW . . .

About the Pronunciation Key and Accent Marks

Write the answer to the question by spelling each word.

A suspected burglar led police on a high-speed chase through a town. The chase lasted twenty minutes, but the police had no trouble following the man. Why?

Bi kôz´ hē pu̇t ôn his tėrn sig´ nel ev´ rē tīm hē mād e tėrn.

Definitions

Many people use a dictionary to find meanings of words. When you look for a meaning, you may find only one definition. Sometimes you may have to read several definitions to find the meaning you want. Some definitions may have several parts.

Suppose you read in a story that a student took a *satchel* to school. What is a satchel? Look below at the entry for *satchel*. How many syllables does the word have? Is the accent on the first or second syllable? Read the definition. Could you put a pair of shoes in a satchel?

---

sar cas tic (sär kas′tik), *adj.* using sarcasm; sneering; cutting: *"Don't hurry!" was his sarcastic comment as I began to dress at my usual slow rate.* —**sar cas′ti cal ly,** *adv.*

sar coph a gus (sär kof′ə gəs), *n., pl.* **-gi** (-jī), **-gus es.** a stone coffin, especially one ornamented with sculpture or inscriptions. [< Greek *sarkophagos*, originally, flesh-eating (stone) < *sarkos* flesh + *phagein* eat]

sar don ic (sär don′ik), *adj.* bitterly sarcastic, scornful, or mocking: *a sardonic outlook.* [< Greek *sardonios*, alteration of *sardanios*, perhaps influenced by *sardonion*, a supposed Sardinian plant that produced hysterical convulsions] —**sar don′i cal ly,** *adv.*

sa ri (sär′ē), *n.* the principal outer garment of Hindu women, a long piece of cotton or silk wrapped around the body, with one end falling nearly to the feet and the other end thrown over the head or shoulder. [< Hindi *sārī* < Sanskrit *śāṭī*]

sa rong (sə rông′, sə rong′), *n.* a rectangular piece of cloth, usually a brightly colored printed material, worn as a skirt by men and women in the Malay Archipelago and certain other islands of the Pacific. [< Malay *sārung*]

sar sa pa ril la (sas′pə ril′ə, sär′sə pə ril′ə), *n.* 1 any of various species of tropical American climbing or trailing greenbriers. 2 the dried roots of any of these plants, formerly used in medicine. 3 a soft drink, usually carbonated, flavored with the root of any of these plants. [< Spanish *zarzaparilla*]

sarong

sas sa fras (sas′ə fras), *n.* 1 a slender eastern North American tree of the same family as the laurel, having fragrant, yellow flowers, bluish-black fruit, and soft, light wood. 2 the aromatic dried bark of its root, used in medicine and to flavor candy, soft drinks, etc. [< Spanish *sasafrás*]

sas sy (sas′ē), *adj.,* **-si er, -si est.** rude. —**sas′si ly,** *adv.* —**sas′si ness,** *n.*

satch el (sach′əl), *n.* a small bag for carrying clothes, books, etc.; handbag. [< Old French *sachel* < Latin *succellus*, diminutive of *succus* sack¹]

Parts of speech and plurals

Dictionary entries show the part of speech. The abbreviations for parts of speech are shown on page 60. Look at the entry for *sari*. What part of speech is *sari*?

An entry may also show how to spell the plural form of a noun. If a plural is formed by adding *-s* or *-es,* it is usually not shown. If a plural is formed in a different way, the spelling is shown. There is no plural shown for *sari.* This means that the plural is formed by adding *-s.*

Now look at the first part of the entry for *sarcophagus.* The plural can be formed with *-gi* or *-guses.*

The explorer found several *sarcophagi.*

or

The explorer found several *sarcophaguses.*

Other forms of a word

Sometimes other forms of a word are shown. Look at the entry for *sassy* on page 63. What part of speech is *sassy*? Notice that two more adjective endings are shown: *-sier* and *-siest*. What form of *sassy* would you use in this sentence?

My sister is the ———————————————— person I know.

What is the noun form of *sassy*? ————————————————

ACTIVITY 9
Understanding dictionary entries

Answer the following questions by looking at the dictionary entries on page 63.

1. What is the adverbial form of *sardonic*? ————————————————————————————

2. What part of speech is *sarsaparilla*? ————————————————————————————

3. Can you drink *sarsaparilla*? ————————————————————————————

4. Is *sarcastic* an adjective? ————————————————————————————

5. What is the plural of *sarong*? ————————————————————————————

6. How many pronunciations are shown for *sarong*? ————————————————————————

7. Would you wear a sarong around your head? ————————————————————————

8. Which meaning of *sassafras* would describe what you might have in your yard?

(Give the number of the definition.) ————————————————————————————

---

sar casm (sär′kaz′əm), *n.* **1** a sneering or cutting remark; ironical taunt. **2** act of making fun of a person to hurt his or her feelings; harsh or bitter irony: *"How unselfish you are!"* said the girl in sarcasm as her brother took the biggest piece of cake. [< Greek *sarkasmos* < *sarkazein* to sneer, strip off flesh < *sarkos* flesh]
➤ **Sarcasm, irony, satire** are often confused, although they are not synonyms. *Sarcasm* is the use of language to hurt, wound, or ridicule: *Why don't you give us your advice since you know everything?* That is also an example of irony, although not all sarcasm is irony nor is all irony sarcasm. *Irony* is the deliberate use of language in a sense opposite to that which the words ordinarily have: *This cloudburst makes a fine day for a picnic. Satire* uses irony and sarcasm to expose and attack vices or follies: *In "Gulliver's Travels" Jonathan Swift makes notable use of satire.*

sar dine (sär dēn′), *n., pl.* **-dines** or **-dine. 1** a young pilchard preserved in oil for food. **2** any of certain similar small fish prepared in the same way. **3 packed like sardines,** very much crowded. [< Latin *sardina* < Greek *sardēnē*, probably originally, Sardinian fish] **—sar dine′like′,** *adj.*

Sar din i a (sär din′ē ə), *n.* **1** large Italian island in the Mediterranean Sea, west of the Italian peninsula. 1,582,000 pop.; 9300 sq. mi. (24,100 sq. km.) **2** former kingdom (1720-1860) that included this island, Savoy, Piedmont, and eventually most of the Italian mainland. **—Sar din′i an,** *adj., n.*

sar to ri al (sär tôr′ē əl, sär tōr′ē əl), *adj.* of tailors or their work: *His clothes were a sartorial triumph.* [< Latin *sartor* tailor, ultimately < *sarcire* to patch] **—sar to′ri al ly,** *adv.*

sa shay (sa shā′), *v.i.* INFORMAL. glide, move, or go about. [alteration of *chassé* a gliding dance step < French]

sa shi mi (sä shē′mē), *n.* a Japanese dish consisting of thin slices of raw fish, usually dipped in a sauce and eaten as an appetizer. [< Japanese]

Sas quatch (sas′kwach), *n.* Bigfoot. [< its American Indian name]

sass (sas), INFORMAL. **—***n.* rudeness; back talk; impudence. **—***v.t.* be rude or disrespectful to. **—***v.i.* talk rudely or impudently. [variant of *sauce*]

Etymologies A dictionary entry may contain an etymology. An etymology tells the history of a word. Look at the entry for *sardine* on page 64. The etymology appears in brackets at the end of the definition. The etymology tells you that the word is from (<) the Latin word *sardina*. This word is from the Greek word *sardēnē*. The word probably meant "Sardinian fish." (Note that the entry following *sardine* tells you about Sardinia.)

Illustrative sentences and usage notes Dictionaries usually include sentences that show how a word is used. The second meaning of *sarcasm* shows a sentence in italic type. It is called an illustrative sentence because it illustrates, or shows, how a word is used.

At the end of the entry for *sarcasm* there is a usage note. This explains the similarities and differences among *sarcasm*, *irony*, and *satire*.

Restrictive labels and idioms Now look at the entry for *sass*. There you see the label INFORMAL. This is called a restrictive label. The label INFORMAL means that the word is common in everyday speech or writing. It is not normally used in formal writing or speech. If you were writing a business letter, you would not use the word *sass*. You could use the word in a friendly letter.

Some entries show idioms. Look again at the entry for *sardine*. The idiom with the entry for sardine is "packed like sardines." Native speakers of a language usually understand idioms. Non-native speakers are sometimes puzzled by idioms. Idioms cannot be understood simply by knowing the meanings of the words in the idiom. Some other examples of English idioms are: *stand a chance, play off, rough it.*

ACTIVITY 10
Understanding dictionary entries

Answer the following questions by looking at the dictionary entries on page 64.

1. What language does *sashimi* come from? _____

2. What is the illustrative sentence for *sartorial*? (Copy it.) _____

3. What is the restrictive label for *sashay*? _____

4. Where is the accent in *sashay*? _____

5. What language does *Sasquatch* come from? _____

6. What is another name for *Sasquatch*? _____

7. Is the sentence below an example of *sarcasm*? _____

Having a flat tire is a wonderful way to start our vacation.

Homographs   Look at the entries for *sash*. Notice the small numbers [1] and [2]. Although these words are pronounced and spelled the same, they have different etymologies. These words are homographs. Which word, sash[1] or sash[2], could you tie around your waist?

> **sash**[1] (sash), *n.* a long, broad strip of cloth or ribbon, worn round the waist or over one shoulder. [< Arabic *shāsh* muslin]
> **sash**[2] (sash), *n.* 1 frame for the glass of a window or door. 2 part or parts of a window that can be moved to open or close a window. [alteration of *chassis*, taken as plural]

People and places   Entries for people and places give you a few basic facts. Birth and death dates are shown for people. Entries will also tell you why the people are well known. Entries for places tell their location and their size.

ACTIVITY 11
Understanding dictionary entries

Answer the following questions about the entries for people and places.

1. When was John Singer Sargent born? _____

2. What was Saroyan's first name? _____

3. Which ocean is the Sargasso Sea part of? _____

4. When did Sargon II die? _____

5. What is the capital of the province of Saskatchewan? _____

> **Sar gas so Sea**   (sär gas′ō),   part of the Atlantic extending from the West Indies northeast to the Azores.
> **Sar gent** (sär′jənt), *n.* **John Singer**, 1856-1925, American portrait painter.
> **Sar gon II** (sär′gon), died 705 B.C., king of Assyria from 722 to 705 B.C.
> — — — — — — — — — — — — —
> **Sa roy an**   (sə roi′ən),   *n.* **William**, 1908-1981, American playwright and short-story writer.
> — — — — — — — — — — — — —
> **Sa skatch e wan** (sa skach′ə won), *n.* 1 province in S central Canada. 947,000 pop.; 251,700 sq. mi. (651,900 sq. km.) *Capital:* Regina. *Abbrev.:* Sask. 2 river flowing from SW Canada into Lake Winnipeg. 1205 mi. (1939 km.)

Synonyms   Look at the entry for *correct*. At the end of the definition is the abbreviation **Syn.** What follows is a synonym study. Words that mean about the same thing are called synonyms. *Correct, accurate,* and *exact* all mean about the same thing. The synonym study explains small differences among the three words. Synonym studies can be helpful in your writing.

> **cor rect** (kə rekt′), *adj.* **1** free from mistakes or faults; right: *the correct answer.* See synonym study below. **2** agreeing with a recognized standard, especially of good taste; proper: *correct manners.* —*v.t.* **1** change to what is right; remove mistakes or faults from: *Correct any misspellings that you find.* **2** alter or adjust to agree with some standard: *correct the reading of a barometer.* **3** point out or mark the errors of; check: *correct test papers.* **4** set right by punishing; find fault with to improve; punish: *correct a child for misbehaving.* **5** counteract or neutralize (something hurtful); cure; overcome; remedy: *Medicine can sometimes correct stomach trouble.* [< Latin *correctum* made straight < *com-* + *regere* to guide] —**cor rect′a ble,** *adj.* —**cor rect′ly,** *adv.* —**cor rect′ness,** *n.* —**cor rec′tor,** *n.*
> **Syn.** *adj.* **1 Correct, accurate, exact** mean without error or mistake. **Correct** adds nothing to that basic meaning: *I gave correct answers to the questions.* **Accurate** emphasizes the careful effort to make something agree exactly with the facts or with a model: *I gave an accurate account of the accident.* **Exact** emphasizes the complete agreement in every detail with the facts or with a model: *The painting is an exact copy of the original.*

ACTIVITY 12
Using a dictionary to check spelling

Many people use a dictionary to find the correct spelling of a word. Use your dictionary to check the spelling of the words below. One word in each pair is spelled correctly. Write out the correct spelling.

1. recommend, reccommend _____

2. accomodate, accommodate _____

3. accumulate, accummulate _____

4. occassion, occasion _____

5. personell, personnel _____

6. benefit, benifit _____

7. nineth, ninth _____

8. vaccuum, vacuum _____

9. omitted, omited _____

10. occurred, occured _____

11. committee, comittee _____

12. valueable, valuable _____

13. seperate, separate _____

14. arrangment, arrangement _____

Use the dictionary entries to answer these questions.

1. Does the first syllable in *bower* rhyme with "cow" or "low"? _____

2. What part of speech is *bower*? _____

3. Which definitions for *bow*[1] have illustrative sentences? _____

4. What does the idiom *bow and scrape* mean? _____

5. After which syllable is the accent in *bouzouki*? _____

6. For whom was the bowie knife named? _____

7. Where is Corregidor? _____

8. Who was Correggio? _____

9. Is Corpus Christi a city in Arizona? _____

10. How do you spell the plural of *bowman*? _____

---

bou zou ki (bü zü′kē), *n.* a stringed instrument that is somewhat like a mandolin and has a very brilliant tone. [< New Greek *mpouzouki*]

bow[1] (bou), *v.i.* **1** bend the head or body in greeting, respect, worship, or submission. **2** give in; submit; yield. —*v.t.* **1** bend (the head or body) in greeting, respect, worship, or submission. **2** express by a bow: *He bowed his approval.* **3** usher with a bow or bows. **4** cause to stoop; bend: *The old man was bowed by age.*
bow and scrape, be too polite or slavish.
bow down, a weigh down: *bowed down with care.* **b** worship.
bow out, a withdraw: *She sprained her wrist and had to bow out of the tennis tournament.* **b** usher out.
—*n.* **1** a bending of the head or body in greeting, respect, worship, or submission. **2 take a bow,** accept praise, applause, etc., for something done.
[Old English *būgan*] —**bow′er,** *n.*

bow ie knife (bō′ē, bü′ē), a heavy hunting knife with a long, single-edged blade, curved near the point, and carried in a sheath. [< Colonel James *Bowie*, 1799-1836, American pioneer who made it popular]

bow er (bou′ər), *n.* **1** shelter of leafy branches. **2** summerhouse or arbor. [Old English *būr* dwelling]

bow man (bō′mən), *n., pl.* **-men.** archer.

— — — — — — — — — — — — — —

Cor pus Chris ti (kôr′pəs kris′tē), **1** feast of the Roman Catholic Church in honor of the Eucharist, celebrated on the first Thursday after Trinity Sunday. **2** city in S Texas. 232,000. [< Latin *corpus Christi* body of Christ]

Cor reg gio (kô rej′ō), *n.* **An to nio Al le gri da** (än tō′-nyō ä lä′grē dä), 1494-1534, Italian painter.

Cor reg i dor (kə reg′ə dôr), *n.* fortified island at the entrance to Manila Bay, Philippines.

SHOW WHAT YOU KNOW . . .

About Dictionaries

Make up a word and write a dictionary entry for it. (1) Show the word divided into syllables; (2) show the pronunciation; (3) write one definition for the word; (4) write an illustrative sentence; and (5) make up an etymology.

Tables of contents

A table of contents lists the chapter names or article titles with page numbers on which they begin in the publication. Unlike an index, this arrangement is not alphabetical. The contents page usually lists items in order of appearance. In this section, you will study several tables of contents. A table of contents gives a preview of all the things in a book or magazine. It also helps you find a specific chapter or article quickly.

Books   A book's table of contents is usually arranged in chapters. Each chapter is numbered in order. Study the following partial contents page of a book. It shows chapters with subsections.

Contents

Chapter numbers ●

Author ●

Chapter title ●

Page number for beginning of chapter ●

The subsections in this ● chapter

Textbook contents may be divided into units or parts. And these may have sections and chapters. A textbook contents page might look like this.

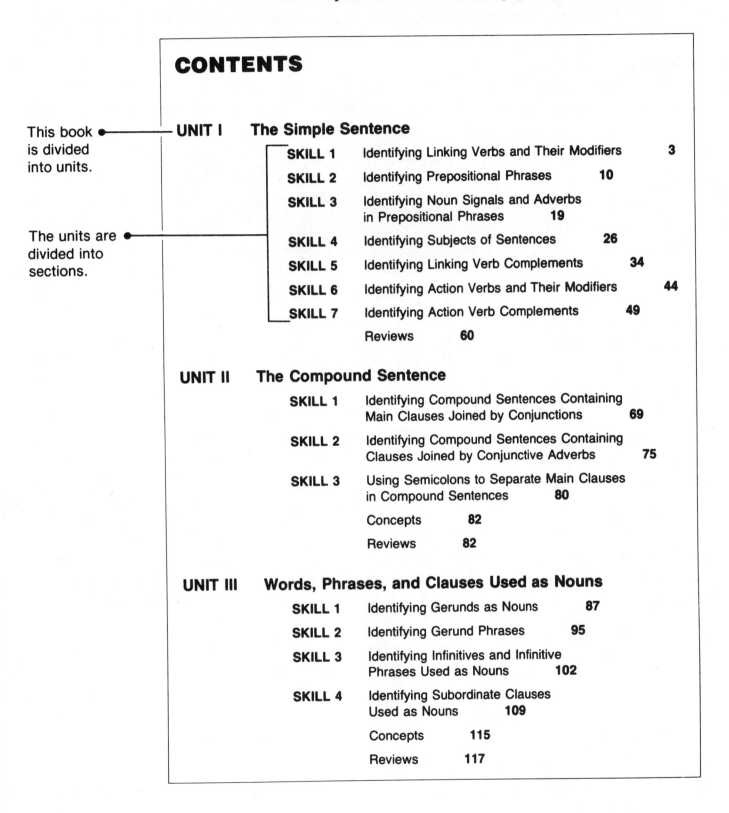

CONTENTS

This book is divided into units.

The units are divided into sections.

This table of contents is divided into units. It also has sections. Use it to answer the questions below.

1. How many units are there on this page? _____

2. What is the title of Unit One?_____

   Unit Two? _____

3. How many pages in this book are about Ralph J. Bunche? _____ Anne Sullivan Macy? _____

4. To which page would you turn to read about Martin Luther King, Jr.? _____ Leonard Bernstein? _____

5. Who was Countee Cullen? _____

6. What science fiction writer is included here? _____

_____

Magazines Information in tables of contents pages may be grouped by subject. Groupings such as "gardening," "decorating," or "crafts" might contain all the articles on those subjects, regardless of where they appear in the magazine. Often the contents of a magazine are shown in the order in which they appear.

Many magazines have sections such as "letters" that appear in every issue. Sometimes these sections are listed under the word *Departments* in the table of contents. Frequently there is a preview of what's coming up in the next issue.

Contents pages can help you decide whether you want to buy a magazine. Subscribers and purchasers of magazines can skim the contents pages to decide what they want to read.

ACTIVITY 14
Using the table of contents of a magazine

Look at the table of contents from the magazine *Consumer Reports* on the facing page. Use the contents page to answer the questions that follow.

1. Is this table of contents arranged by subject groupings or by the order in which the articles appear? _____

2. Indicate whether the following features are in *Consumer Reports* every month or are included in this month only by putting a check in the correct column.

	Every Month	**This Month**
a. Pocket Guide to Money	_____	_____
b. Movies	_____	_____
c. Electric fans	_____	_____
d. Wasted health-care dollars	_____	_____
e. Which tea is best?	_____	_____

3. On what page does the article on hand vacuums start? _____

4. How many teas did the tea tasters sample? _____

5. How many kinds of autos will be featured in future issues? _____

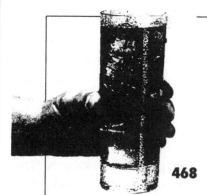

IN THIS ISSUE

July 1992   Volume 57, No. 7

468

435

415

DEPARTMENTS

IN FUTURE ISSUES

Auto insurance Next month, Ratings of the best and worst auto insurers, plus ways to save money on your insurance.

Autos Acura Legend, Audi 100, Mazda 929, Volvo 960 **Home** Household insect control ■ Washing machines ■ Food processors ■ Vinyl floor coverings **Personal** Business suits ■ Blow dryers ■ Mouthwashes ■ Electric toothbrushes ■ Toothpastes **Health and fitness** Ratings of HMOs ■ A look at Canada's health-care system ■ Tennis racquets **Food** Low-fat ice cream ■ Seltzer

Study the following textbook contents page. Notice that it has a number of divisions. Then answer the questions .

Contents

1. The contents page on page 75 shows two main divisions. What are these two divisions?

   _____

2. Chapter 1 is divided into four subsections. What are they?

   _____

3. On what page does the subsection called "Run-on Sentences" begin? _____

4. What is the title of Section 2? _____

5. How many pages are there in the subsection on "Making a Journal Entry"? _____

6. What can be found on page 51? _____

7. If you wanted to learn how to write a personal letter, what chapter would you read? _____

8. What is the title of Part 1? _____

9. How many divisions or subsections are there in Chapter 3? _____

10. How many chapters are there in Section 1? _____

Indexes

WORDS TO KNOW

classification number   the number of a section of classified ads, not a page number

index   an alphabetical list of the subjects in a book

subject   the name of an item in an index; a topic

subtopic or subentry   an entry in an index that is secondary to the main topic, such as elementary schools under the main topic of schools

topic   the name of an item in an index; a subject

Book indexes   A book index is in the back of a book. It lists people, titles, or topics alphabetically. It gives page numbers where you will find these entries. This makes finding information easier. Most textbooks have an index. Look at the following book index.

Alphabetical arrangement
of the entries

Index

Book title •————————

Author •————————

Page on which this •————————
item can be found

Topic found in this book •————

Subtopics •————

Notice the alphabetical arrangement of people, topics, and subtopics. An index should list every page on which a topic appears. Of course, not every word in a book appears in the index. Most often you find key words, key people or places, special terms, and general topics discussed in that book.

ACTIVITY 15
Using a book index

Study the following book index and answer the questions about it.

Index

1. On what pages do you find complex sentences? _____

2. On what page will you find the word "couplet"? _____

3. How many pages does Chief Joseph appear on? _____

4. What pages deal with Jimmy Carter? _____

5. What page(s) should you turn to if you want to read about American Indian dances? _____

popular dances? _____

ballet? _____

Catalog indexes

Catalogs have indexes, too. A catalog index lists the items you can order. It also lists the pages where you can find these items.

Like all indexes, the catalog index is alphabetical. Most people use a catalog index when they want a certain item. For example, Bobby Goldstein wants to order a new basketball. He just got the mail-order catalog. Bobby turns to the index on page 80. He looks under the Bs for "Basketball." He finds "Basketballs . . . . 233."

ACTIVITY 16

Using a catalog index

Use the catalog index on page 80 to answer these questions:

• First, use the "Find-It-Fast Index" to complete the chart below:

Type of Product	Pages	
	From	To
Appliances	_____	_____
Giftware	_____	_____
Watches	_____	_____
Tools	_____	_____
Jewelry	_____	_____
Home Entertainment	_____	_____

Index

- Use the main index on the previous page to find the specific items below:

Item	Page(s)	Item	Page(s)
Fondue Pots		Frying Pans	
Drip Coffee Makers		Salad Bowls	
Cookie Jars		Blenders	
Humidifiers		Calculators	
Electric Brooms		Movie Cameras	
Clothes Hampers		Barbells	
Fire Extinguishers		Ironing Boards	

CHECK YOUR UNDERSTANDING OF INDEXES

Following is the first page of a yellow pages index from a telephone book. Study it carefully. Then answer the questions about it:

On which page would you look if . . .

1. you needed a dentist? _____

2. you were trying to locate a non-denominational church? _____

3. you wanted to find a dealer to buy your coin collection? _____

4. you wanted to find a chiropractor? _____

5. you were trying to find a place to buy a part for your car? _____

6. you wanted to find all the bicycle stores in the area? _____

7. you wanted to find the number to call for a bus schedule? _____

8. you wanted a listing of the campgrounds in the area? _____

9. you wanted to get your hair styled? _____

10. you wanted to rent a boat? _____

This is your YELLOW PAGES
INDEX
(ALPHABETICALLY ARRANGED)

Reading Critically

ACTIVITY 1—Reading Ads Carefully (p. 3)
Lose Fat Forever Ad
1. Answers will vary.
2. Answers will vary.

Career Certificate Ad
1. no
2. a box number
3. typing, auto mechanics, truck driving, hair styling, catering, barbering, computer programming, driver instructor training
4. Answers will vary.
5. a high school dropout; a high school graduate with no vocational skills; an adult who never attended high school
6. • When you finish the course, your "Career Certificate" will help you get a job.
   • Many people who take a career course earn $50,000 a year.
   • You don't have to worry about money now. The important thing is to enroll for the current semester. You can always pay later.
   • The training is like college. (There are semesters, registration, tuition fees.)

ACTIVITY 2—Reading Ads with Emotional Appeal (p. 6)
1. **Intelligent Shoppers Ad:** b
2. **Hair Color Magic Ad:** c

ACTIVITY 3—Reading Ads with Emotional Appeal— "The Famous Person" (p. 7)
1. Answers will vary
2. • I know about *all cars* . . . your car, your brother's car, your mother's car, your Aunt Isabelle's car, my car.
   • . . . and I'm tellin' you what your car needs is PST.
   • Put PST in your car and you'll run like a champion!
   • Use PST in your car and it'll be ready for the Indiana 600 . . .
3. b (a is also acceptable)

ACTIVITY 4—Reading Ads with Emotional Appeal— "Get on the Bandwagon" (p. 8)
1. • Everyone, but Everyone, is chewing Minty-Fresh Gum!
   • Join the crowd!
   • Try it!
2. The drawing shows a variety of people.
3. Answers will vary. Students should mention making up one's mind is desirable.

ACTIVITY 5—Reading Ads—Specific Information or Glowing Generality? (p. 9)
1. Specific information
2. Glowing generality
3. Glowing generality
4. Specific information
5. Specific information
6. Glowing generality

ACTIVITY 6—Evaluating Popular Advertisements: Finding Out What Types of Ads Appeal to You (p. 10)
Sweet Dreams Ad
1. Answers will vary.
2. Answers will vary.
3. (a) "What would it be like to make the cheerleading squad . . . or win the Olympics . . . or become the most popular girl *ever*?"
   (b) if you ever dream about . . . winning beauty contests; Sweet Dreams make my dreams come true.
   (c) Every one of them lets me see my dreams come true; If you ever dream about boys, winning beauty contests and becoming famous . . .; You've *got* to read them so you, too, can see *your* dreams come true!

Lustra-Curl Ad
1. vanity—need to look good (also bandwagon appeal—need to follow the crowd)
2. perfect curls; finest in after-care products
3. Lustrasilk makes at least twelve after-care products (as pictured); Lustrasilk recommends that you ask you hair stylist about the after-care products shown.

4. The Lustra-Curl is the "real curl"; Lustra-Curl gives you versatility for lots of styles; You'll have all the fun . . .

Buf-Oxal Ad
Facts
   • Buf-Oxal is a benzoyl peroxide gel.
   • Buf-Oxal is available in 5% and 10% strengths.
   • Buf-Oxal is water-based.
Opinions
   • Zits are the pits.
   • Buf-Oxal is gentle.
   • You will be surprised at how quickly Buf-Oxal will clean up your pimples, blackheads, and blemishes.

Check Your Understanding of Advertisements (p. 14)
1. guarantee
2. glowing generality
3. vanity
4. bandwagon appeal
5. optional
6. endorse
7. emotional appeal
8. glowing generality
9. not truthful and half-truths
10. sense appeal

SHOW WHAT YOU KNOW... About Advertisements (p. 15)
Answers will vary.

ACTIVITY 7—Interpreting Magazine Subscription Offers (p. 17)
1. T
2. T
3. T
4. T
5. F

ACTIVITY 8—Reading a CD Offer for Details (p. 19)
1. $1.86
2. every four weeks; up to six times per year
3. nothing
4. indicate your preference on the card and mail it back by the date specified
5. 10 days
6. yes
7. yes
8. the club
9. $12.98-$15.98; $6.95
10. after you have completed your membership agreement (to buy 6 more selections anytime during the next three years)

ACTIVITY 9—Reading a Book Club Offer for Details (p. 20)
1. four
2. $2 plus shipping and handling costs
3. 10
4. yes; there is a shipping and handling cost
5. 15 times a year (about every $3\frac{1}{2}$ weeks)
6. four
7. mark the reply form and return it by the specified date

ACTIVITY 10—Reading Coupon Offers (p. 21)
1. Cheerios cereal; Bold Hold hair spray
2. Cheerios: yes, 10 oz. or larger; Bold Hold: no
3. no
4. Bold Hold: yes, 2/28/93; Cheerios: yes 3/15/88

ACTIVITY 11—Reading Refund and Free Coupon Offers (p. 22)
Burger King Coupon
1. $1.00
2. no
3. no
4. 11

Mail-In Certificate
1. $2.00 cash refund
2. yes; UPC symbols from any 3 Betty Crocker products listed on the coupon and the coupon itself
3. $2.00 in cash
4. General Mills, Inc., Box 5237, Minneapolis, MN 55460

5. up to 6 weeks
6. May 31, 1988

Check Your Understanding of Special Offers (p. 23)
1. coupon
2. expiration date
3. obligation
4. refund
5. discount
6. redeem
7. T
8. T
9. T
10. F

SHOW WHAT YOU KNOW... About Special Offers (p. 24)
Answers will vary.

Understanding Agreements and Warranties

ACTIVITY 1—Using Credit Terms (p. 27)
1. installment
2. interest
3. percentage rate
4. disclosure
5. creditor
6. down payment
7. co-maker
8. default
9. delinquent
10. debts

ACTIVITY 2—Reading Credit Agreements (p. 27)
1. c
2. c (a is also acceptable)
3. c
4. c

ACTIVITY 3—Using Agreements and Contract Words (p. 28)
A. 3
B. 2
C. 7
D. 8
E. 9
F. 1
G. 10
H. 6
I. 5
J. 4

ACTIVITY 4—Reading Terms on Charge Accounts (p. 29)
1. F
2. T
3. T
4. F
5. T
6. T
7. T
8. T
9. T
10. F

ACTIVITY 5—Reading Agreements (p. 30)
1. c
2. f
3. f
4. a
5. c
6. d
7. e
8. e
9. b
10. a

Check Your Understanding of Agreements and Contracts (p. 33)
1. c
2. a
3. a
4. a
5. b
6. b
7. b
8. b
9. a
10. c

SHOW WHAT YOU KNOW... About Agreements and Contracts (p. 34)
Answers will vary.

ACTIVITY 6—Using Warranty Words (p. 36)
1. H
2. E
3. F
4. A
5. C
6. B
7. G
8. D

ACTIVITY 7—Using Warranty Words (p. 36)
1. manufacturer
2. full warranty
3. limited warranty
4. prepaid
5. defects; authorized dealer

ACTIVITY 8—Reading Warranties for Details (p. 37)
1. Sharp CB
2. Sharp Electronics Corp., 10 Keystone Place, Paramus, NJ 07651
3. defects in workmanship and materials
4. one year
5. return it to the manufacturer at address on warranty

ACTIVITY 9—Reading Warranties for Details (p. 38)
1. F
2. T
3. F
4. T
5. F
6. F
7. T
8. F
9. T
10. T

ACTIVITY 10—Reading a Car Warranty (p. 39)
What Is Covered
1. c
2. d
3. d
4. c
What Is Not Covered
1. Any combination of three of the following is acceptable: collision, fire, theft, freezing, vandalism, riot, explosion, objects striking the car, driving over curbs, overloading, racing or other competition, alterations to the car
2. Any combination of two of the following is acceptable: airborne fallout (chemicals, tree sap, etc.), stones, hail, earthquake, water or flood, windstorm, lightning
3. the owner (buyer)
4. The Maintenance Schedule and Owner's Manual explain when maintenance is needed.

Check Your Understanding of Warranties (p. 41)
1. c
2. a
3. b
4. c

5. c
6. a
7. a
8. b
9. b
10. b

SHOW WHAT YOU KNOW... About Warranties (p. 42)
Answers will vary.

Reference Strategies

ACTIVITY 1—Using the Card Catalog (p. 45)
1. Br-Ch
2. O-Pe
3. U-Z
4. Bi-Bo
5. Pe-Pi
6. Ri-So
7. Ch-D
8. A-Bei
9. Ri-So
10. Pe-Pi
11. Te-U
12. Ch-D
13. L
14. E-G
15. M

ACTIVITY 2—Using a Computer (p. 49)
1. Witch
2. Jane
3. Brontë
4. Austen
5. Old
6. Doyle
7. Kerr
8. Simon
9. Raisin
10. David

ACTIVITY 3—Using the Dewey Decimal System (p. 51)
1. 800–899
2. 100–199
3. 800–899
4. 700–799
5. 500–599
6. 500–599
7. 900–999
8. 600–699
9. 200–299
10. 400–499

ACTIVITY 4—Using the *Readers' Guide* (p. 54)
1. Any two of the following: Beatles, Chipmunks, Disco groups, Phonograph records—Rock music, Rock musicians
2. Abba: Ready for the Fortune 500
3. Hi Fi (*High Fidelity*)
4. *Teen*
5. Nov. 27, 1980
6. Chipmunks (recording group)
7. J. Farber; yes
8. November and December
9. 13
10. yes

Check Your Understanding of Reference Strategies (p. 55)
1. T
2. T
3. T
4. T
5. T
6. F
7. F
8. T

9. F
10. F

SHOW WHAT YOU KNOW... About Reference Works (p. 55)
Answers will vary. Students should be encouraged to become familiar with using the almanac, gazetteer, and world atlas.

ACTIVITY 5—Locating Words in a Dictionary (p. 57)
compete
competency
competitive
complacence
complacency
complex
point
position
posse
possess
possessed
postage

ACTIVITY 6—Using Guide Words (p. 59)

hilt/hold	holder/hooky	hooligan/houseboat
history	homework	horoscope
hogwash	honey	hostage
hoax	honest	hotshot
hives	hole	horror
hint	homage	hospital

ACTIVITY 7—Using the Pronunciation Key (p. 61)
Answers will vary.

ACTIVITY 8—Using the Pronunciation Key and Accent Marks (p. 63)
1. cinema
2. classical
3. complication
4. encyclopedia
5. Florida
6. Houston
7. jaw
8. joy
9. bilingual
10. thyme
11. though
12. whim

SHOW WHAT YOU KNOW... About the Pronunciation Key and Accent Marks (p. 62)
Because he put on his turn signal every time he made a turn.

ACTIVITY 9—Understanding Dictionary Entries (p. 64)
1. sardonically
2. noun
3. yes
4. yes
5. sarongs
6. two
7. no
8. 1

ACTIVITY 10—Understanding Dictionary Entries (p. 65)
1. Japanese
2. His clothes were a sartorial triumph.
3. Informal
4. after the second syllable
5. American Indian
6. Bigfoot
7. Yes

ACTIVITY 11—Understanding Dictionary Entries (p. 66)
1. 1856
2. William
3. Atlantic
4. 705 B.C.
5. Regina

ACTIVITY 12—Using the Dictionary to Check Spelling (p. 67)
1. recommend
2. accommodate
3. accumulate
4. occasion
5. personnel
6. benefit
7. ninth
8. vacuum
9. omitted
10. occurred
11. committee
12. valuable
13. separate
14. arrangement

Check Your Understanding of Dictionaries (p. 68)
1. cow
2. noun
3. 2; 4
4. be too polite or slavish
5. after the second syllable
6. Colonel James Bowie
7. at the entrance to Manila Bay, Philippines
8. an Italian painter
9. no, it's a city in Texas
10. bowmen

SHOW WHAT YOU KNOW... About Dictionaries (p. 69)
Answers will vary. Students should be encouraged to use their imaginations in coining new words and meanings.

ACTIVITY 13—Using the Table of Contents of a Book (p. 72)
1. four
2. Courage Was Their Companion; "I Have a Dream"
3. 12; 11
4. 66; 118
5. a poet
6. Isaac Asimov

ACTIVITY 14—Using the Table of Contents of a Magazine (p. 73)
1. order in which the articles appear
2. a. every month
   b. every month
   c. this month
   d. this month
   e. this month
3. 451
4. 78
5. 4

Check Your Understanding of Contents Pages (p. 75)
1. Section 1 and Section 2
2. Using Vivid Words; Nouns and Verbs; Adjectives and Adverbs; Intensifiers
3. 28
4. Personal Writing: Writing for Yourself
5. two
6. Planning Your Life Story
7. Chapter 7
8. Let's Write!
9. six
10. four

ACTIVITY 15—Using a Book Index (p. 78)
1. 237–239
2. 21
3. three
4. 89–91
5. 39–42; 36–38; 43–45

ACTIVITY 16—Using a Catalog Index (p. 79)
"Find-it-Fast Index"
1. 154–174
2. 103–126

3. 80–93
4. 175–179
5. 4–79
6. 241–252
Main Index
7. 168
8. 160
9. 103
10. 173
11. 190, 191
12. 143, 224
13. back cover
14. 133, 134, 137, 158
15. 118
16. 167
17. 216–218, 250
18. 209
19. 235
20. 155

Check Your Understanding of Indexes (p. 81)
1. 34
2. 31
3. 33
4. 28
5. 3 (or 5)
6. 16
7. 20
8. 20
9. 12 (Both "Barbers" and "Beauty Salons" are on p. 12.)
10. 18